DYING

WAS THE

BEST THING

THAT EVER

HAPPENED TO ME

DYING

WAS THE

BEST THING

THAT EVER

HAPPENED TO ME

Stories of Healing and Wisdom
Along Life's Journey

WILLIAM E. HABLITZEL, MD

SUNSHINE RIDGE PUBLISHING

Published in the United States by Sunshine Ridge Publishing

Submit all requests for reprinting to:
Greenleaf Book Group LP
4425 Mopac South, Suite 600
Longhorn Bldg., 3rd Floor
Austin, TX 78735
(512) 891-6100

Publisher's Cataloging in Publication data
Hablitzel, William E.
Dying was the best thing that ever happened to me: stories of healing and wisdom along life's journey / William E. Hablitzel.
p. cm.
LCCN 2005937062
1. Physician and patient—Anecdotes. 2. Medicine—Anecdotes. 3. Spiritual life. I. Title.
R727.3.H3122 2006   610.69'6
QBI05-600202

ISBN 10: 0-9772185-1-1
ISBN 13: 978-09772185-1-6

First Edition
Printed in the United States of America

09 08 07 06   10 9 8 7 6 5 4 3 2 1

To Caroline, who helped me see a different path upon which to walk.

To Ken and Kathy, who shared their path with me.

And to my father, for shining light upon the way.

Contents

Foreword

Throughout my life, I've considered books to be some of my closest friends, strange as that may seem. In moments of great distress, I have found myself reaching for a book and opening it to a page—any page—to start reading. There is a magical, mystical quality to a good book. It gives you an opportunity to listen to the author speak to you personally and share with you whatever seems important. At the end of your reading, you may even think of the author as a teacher, a mentor, a guide, or even more important, an old friend who shares wisdom and insight.

When I received a copy of Dr. William Hablitzel's manuscript, *Dying Was the Best Thing That Ever Happened to Me*, I decided that I was going to look at it as soon as I got a chance. Now, you must understand that I get tons of books from people who want me to read their manuscripts and make a comment. Much as I'd love to, I would be spending my every waking moment reading if I did that. But once in a while, once in a long, long while, a certain book grabs me by the throat and will not let me go until I decide to sit down and read it immediately.

So it was with Bill's book. The haunting title and the urge to find out what it meant combined to make me put aside all my other time commitments and to start reading. And that was the beginning of a whole new, glorious adventure. I kept reading and could not stop until the early hours of the morning when I had turned the last page. There was a sense of freedom and hope, coupled with a slight sadness. The sense of freedom and hope came from what I read in the book; the sadness was because I had come to the end and there was no more to be read. Any author who can do that to a reader is a master of the art and science of writing.

In his book, Bill combines his experience as a great physician and teacher with rare wisdom and insight to create a brilliant guide for life and living. And he does this with beautiful, yet simple, words. Many of my good friends are physicians so I am used to their complex ways of writing way above the head of the common person. Not so with Bill, the author, and Bill, the doctor. Somehow the two blend into one as words of comfort, hope, and mystery flow onto paper.

This book brings new meaning to the words *dying* and *living*. The stories told here are true and came from Bill's special experiences as a physician who has seen much and who wanted to make a difference in his corner of the universe. There is a great temptation for me to tell you a bit about the stories in this book. But I will refrain from doing so. I do not want to deprive you, the reader, of the pleasure of discovery as you go through the pages. After all, I was privileged to explore and discover for myself the beauty and wisdom, the joy and sadness, the mystery and the magic of this special book.

The late great Dr. Elisabeth Kübler-Ross, author of the classic book *On Death and Dying*, was a very close friend of mine. I was the vice president of the Elisabeth Kübler-Ross Center for a number of years until her retirement. Many an evening, after dinner, we would sit in her living room and discuss the meaning of life, death, and the afterlife. Sometimes, those discussions would go very late into the night, and they were always exciting and "learningful." I would never presume to say that I know exactly what she would have thought about this book, but since I knew her so well, I cannot help but think that she would have smiled and said, "What a wonderful book! It should be read by every inhabitant of this planet."

Do not only buy this book for yourself. Get a copy for someone near and dear to you. You'll be glad you did. Keep your copy in a safe place and read it often. Beware of lending it to others because, I assure you, the chances of having it returned are slim. You'll want to return again and again to the moving, true stories that are contained within.

Thank you, Bill. Thank you for sharing this wonderful work with all of us. Thank you for showing us the compassionate heart of a true doctor. I must warn you, however, that after your readers complete this volume, they will clamor for more and you might find yourself in the middle of a sequel to further the insights you've provided here. I, for one, will keep pestering you until you sit down and write more—hopefully, many more—books like this one.

John Harricharan
Award-winning author of *When You Can Walk on Water, Take the Boat*
www.Insight2000.com

Introduction

There are moments in life powerful enough to change us instantly and forever. Far too often, though, these special moments come when we are not present to notice, lost in the dramas of yesterday or our plans for tomorrow. Perhaps wisdom is living the richness that each day offers, being present to recognize those moments with the power to transform us, and seizing them before they can slip away into the currents of time.

We live in a complicated and confusing world. We struggle to understand natural disasters of unprecedented scale, unimaginable human cruelty carried out in the name of religion, and vast plagues of want and scarcity. The newspapers that we read, the television that we watch, and the music that we listen to provides a bottomless well of fear and worry from which we are free to draw. Our days have become hectic, with too much to do and too little time to do it. We are so busy making a living that many of us, perhaps most of us, have forgotten how to live.

In those special moments, however, confusion can clear to understanding, fear can melt away to peace, and scarcity can turn into abundance. We can be touched by the realization that what we have long looked for has found us. Such is the power of the lives that surround us.

Physicians are entrusted within the lives of their patients, lives woven from the threads of spirituality, touched by the mysteries of the universe, and filled with stories to tell. These stories can teach the secrets of a life filled with meaning, of wisdom, and of extraordinary journeys. They are sacred lessons, far too precious to be hidden away in the sterility of the hospital and the coldness of the examination room. They are lessons that teach of a miraculous place and shine light on the path that will take us there.

The people that you will meet within these pages are real. Although their names and circumstances have been changed to preserve their privacy, the essence of their being and the magic that springs from their lives has been faithfully reproduced. They are souls that have blessed my journey—and they have helped me realize just how important our brief time here is. They have been my teachers. I invite you to learn from them as well, and join me on an incredible voyage to a place few people see and fewer still come to know.

It will be wondrous!

William E. Hablitzel, MD

DYING

WAS THE

BEST THING

THAT EVER

HAPPENED TO ME

CHAPTER 1

I Did Not Start to Live
Until I Started to Die

When the student is ready, the teacher will appear.
ANCIENT BUDDHIST PROVERB

My earilest days as a physician found me in a strange city, away from the security of home for the first time, and filled with both excitement and apprehension for the journey that lay ahead. The title *doctor* fit much like a new pair of shoes—looking polished to the eye, but feeling uncomfortable and needing wear. Being addressed as "Doctor" would invariably cause me to look about in search of a real physician.

Although the memory of medical school graduation was still fresh and vivid, I held no illusions that those years of study had adequately prepared me for the practice of medicine. I had much to learn and I was in a rush, almost a panic, to do so. As I started internship, I knew that the learning had just begun. It was a different kind of learning. Morning rounds, grand rounds, afternoon rounds—endless hours of rounding and learning patient care firsthand from more experienced physicians. Internship was saturated with the opportunity to learn. Sometimes, the most powerful lessons were those taught by the most unlikely teachers, the patients we cared for.

Much of my training as an intern took place during rotations through our local VA hospital. The VA hospital was a great place to learn medicine. It was a bottomless well of those in need, and at the end of the day, even the most inexperienced among us felt the satisfaction of service. It was also an intimidating place, and frustration was an emotion we were taught to master from the moment we walked through the doors. That moment, my first glimpse of the VA hospital, will remain seared in my memory forever.

No signage was necessary to identify the building as government designed and operated. It would have been difficult to build a more drab and uninspired structure. With its concrete block walls and paucity of windows, it could have been a prison. Even the large revolving doors spoke of purpose —the rapid movement of people. Those doors opened into a vast, cavernous space. It was not space dedicated to welcome, or even comfort. It was designed for waiting, and it was well used. Windows were spaced along the perimeter of the room. Above each window a sign described the activity that took place there—benefit services, pharmacy services, emergency services, inpatient registration, outpatient clinics, and even pastoral care. A line of men stretched from each window. Certain windows seemed strategically placed to accommodate impressively long lines. Pharmacy, benefits, and outpatient registration seemed to be particularly popular, with hundreds of men waiting their turn for a moment of individuality. In the center of the room were clustered rows of molded plastic chairs, more typical of a bus station than a hospital. Here veterans waited their turn to stand in line and wait.

It took me a good number of minutes to process the scene before me on that first visit, standing just inside the revolving doors, no doubt with mouth agape. It would not be the last time that day that I would question the wisdom of the path I had selected. How easy it would have been to go back through the doors to a place of safety, familiarity, and comfort. But there was also something fascinating about this strange new world that I had stumbled upon. As I stood among a sea of fathers and grandfathers, I could see my own father and feel his wisdom. He had helped me acquire the title of doctor. What better place to learn to become one?

If I had had any fantasies that my days would be consumed with scholarly pursuits and practicing the art of medicine, the VA system was quick to show me reality. It was a hard place for an intern. Many of the support services taken for granted in the community hospital were lacking or absent at the VA. Medical students and interns were an irresistible and well-exploited resource for budget-strapped VA hospital administrators.

Much to our chagrin, drawing blood, starting IVs, transporting patients for testing, and even clerical and nursing duties would fill the majority of those early days as doctors. Perhaps, though we were too tired and harried to appreciate it, our daily burdens brought us closer to our patients. It was a humbling revelation that patients would share things with their transporter or phlebotomist that they would never dream of telling their doctor. It was through these eyes that patients were transformed into fathers and grandfathers, men with lives to share and lessons to teach. While it would take many years for me to realize, I encountered my greatest teachers while pushing a stretcher or changing a bed. And so it was with Roger Harrold.

I met Mr. Harrold for the first time in the Patient Evaluation Area, the VA's version of the emergency room. His weathered skin and coarse features made him appear older than his sixty-two years. His eyes and soft-spoken way reflected a kind and gentle being, but in those eyes was also a sense of darkness, perhaps even sadness. He had the look of surrender about him, as if his very presence was an admission of personal failure. This was a man unaccustomed to illness and problems that he could not solve himself.

Standing by his side was a petite lady with graying hair and facial lines that suggested a perpetual smile. There was no smile that day, only a look of concern, a look that explained her husband's presence at the hospital. He would have preferred toughing things out at home a while longer, but she couldn't bear the changes that had taken place in her husband of forty years. Not having a family doctor—Mr. Harrold held strong opinions about such things—she had loaded him up in the family car and driven the hundred-some miles to the VA hospital. It was a first for her. He was always the driver.

Mrs. Harrold seemed almost relieved to tell their story. They had lived on a small farm since his discharge from the service after the Second World War. It was a hard life, but one that they savored. She had begun to notice changes in her husband six months, perhaps a year earlier. The changes were so gradual and his denials so unbending that it was easy for them to convince each other that all was well. As time went on, it took longer and longer for Mr. Harrold to complete his morning chores. He stopped sleeping in their bed at night, feeling more comfortable sitting up in a chair. His breathing had become progressively more labored with activity. She had known something was terribly wrong that morning when he was too winded to brush his teeth.

The story line was a familiar one, even for a young intern, and it did not take long to make a diagnosis. It was a diagnosis that a junior medical student should be able to make. Low blood pressure, rapid heart rate, fluid in the lungs and tissues, and decreased oxygen in the bloodstream all spelled congestive heart failure. It was also a problem that a medical student could manage, and it did not take long to place Mr. Harrold on oxygen, start an IV, and administer diuretics to start removing fluid from his system. Within an hour Mr. Harrold felt dramatically better and doctors had earned some credibility in his eyes—this young doctor in particular. I was grateful for the illusion of competency that an easy diagnosis and a simple management plan can provide.

As I pushed Mr. Harrold in a wheelchair to his room, we started to get to know each other. I won some points when he learned that my father was raised on a farm and that he had instilled in me a love of the land and of nature. He spoke of his farm, the crops he raised, and his favorite spot—a pond next to a woodlot frequented by songbirds and waterfowl. We both liked birds. It would become a strong bond between us, probably stronger than that between patient and physician.

Mr. Harrold and I spent a lot of time together over the ensuing days. Every four hours I would appear at his bedside to inject more diuretics into his IV, listen to his chest, and take his blood pressure. There would always be talk. He would tell me all about the birds on his farm, and I would share my stories with him. His favorite bird was the Carolina wren because it would sing during every month of the year, even in the dead of winter. It was a philosophy he admired and thought wise to emulate.

Work at the VA was pendular, one moment engaged in matters of life and death, the next saturated in the absurd. It was easy to miss the drama that swirled about us constantly, and I cherished those slow moments that provided the opportunity to observe. It was like watching excited boys at summer camp, complete with uniforms, activities, and buddies to share stories with. The VA uniform, issued at time of admission, was light brown pajamas with a dark brown robe and slippers. Street clothes and personal items were locked away in the property room until discharge. The day was highly structured for the campers. Each morning patients were told when and where to report for scheduled tests and what times they were required to be in their rooms. But there was also time for play, and groups of men would huddle together to enjoy war stories, each more heroic and horrific than the one before.

Just as every summer camp had a boy that went it alone, the VA had Roger Harrold. He seldom shared in the camaraderie, avoided discussions of war and heroes, and never had a story to tell of his time in the service. I knew that there must be a story hidden behind the darkness of those eyes.

As days stretched into weeks the early improvements won in Mr. Harrold's health were gradually surrendered, and the tide of battle seemed to be turning against us. His heart had been severely damaged by a series of silent and unrecognized heart attacks. Not much heart muscle remained to maintain vital organs. The pump was gradually failing, functioning at barely 10 percent of normal. Increasingly higher doses of medication were required to keep fluid from his lungs, and my visits to his room became more frequent and more urgent. With each visit it became harder to look upon Mr. Harrold as a patient. His wife and son visited nearly every day, and I began to look forward to seeing them as much as he did. Often, we shared dinner together in the VA canteen. It did not take long for Mrs. Harrold to declare the food unfit, and she never came to the hospital without dinner again. She made my nutrition her personal business, and I was always paged when it was time to join them for something to eat. Over homemade soup, sandwiches, and countless baked delicacies, we solved the world's problems, shared joys and sorrows, and traveled a special path together. We had become family.

Harvest season arrived, and for the first time, the corn was taken off the fields without Mr. Harrold. But I believe that he was there in spirit, supervising every step. He wanted to be home by Thanksgiving to see his grandsons again, but it was not to be. As his heart function worsened, his kidneys began to fail. His liver followed next. On morning rounds the day before Thanksgiving, the senior resident asked if I wanted him to tell Mr. Harrold that he was dying. It was something that I had never done before. While I was uncertain of my ability, I knew that the news would best come from me. We decided to give his family their holiday. I would tell him Friday morning.

Ed Harrold was Roger's only child. He was a year younger than me, but already had two children, eight- and six-year-old boys. I liked him immediately and we enjoyed many conversations over coffee during the months that his father was hospitalized. He lived with his wife and sons about an hour from the farm where he was raised. While his father wanted him to take over the family farm, his passion took him in another direction, but the farm remained dear to his heart. The boys spent countless days walking the fields with their grandfather, learning a love for nature. The boys had become Roger's life.

Children were forbidden at the VA hospital, and it seemed unlikely that special dispensation would be considered, even for a dying man. Another VA principle, albeit an unofficial one, is that it is better to ask forgiveness than permission. When the head nurse left the floor for lunch on

Thanksgiving Day, Ed and I sneaked the boys up the back stairs. The boys accomplished what I was unable to do with medications. For that hour, Mr. Harrold was filled with life and happiness. For that hour, he had indeed made it home for Thanksgiving.

I walked the boys downstairs to their mother, leaving Ed and Mrs. Harrold to have some private time with Roger. In the lobby the eldest boy stopped, looked me in the eye, and asked, "Will Gramps go away soon?"

Taken aback, I asked, "Who told you that your grandfather was going away?"

"Gramps did," the boy explained. "He told us that he was going to Heaven and that we wouldn't be able to see him for a long time."

"How does that make you feel?" I inquired with a cracking voice.

"Sad," he said, "but Gramps said that we could walk and talk with him whenever we wanted to at the farm."

As I struggled for a response, their mother nodded at me, and I told them, "Yes, your grandfather will go away soon, but he loves you very much, and he will always be nearby."

Returning to Mr. Harrold's room, it was obvious that everyone had been crying. Feeling awkward, I tried to slip out unnoticed, but Mr. Harrold called me back. He was talking about the war. He had been on the beaches of Normandy. He spoke of numbing fear, of watching friends die, of hearing men cry for their mothers. He spoke of the guilt he felt for having lived, and of the drive to make that life special, a legacy to those he left behind. This had been his secret, the darkness in those eyes.

There was a quiet place at the VA, a seldom-used conference room that I stumbled across during my early days of work. Its soft lighting and comfortable chairs provided precious sanctuary during times of stress. Its best feature was the large window that looked out over bird feeders hung from a tree by the groundskeeper. Early Friday morning, I pushed Mr. Harrold's wheelchair up to that window. We delighted in the red-bellied woodpeckers, the nuthatches, and the titmice, birds that would brighten the dark days of winter and remind us how easily beauty can be found when it is sought.

In the peace of that special place we talked about family, and about love. We contemplated things of beauty, and things that bring meaning. We spoke of life, and of death. He wanted no heroics, no technology, and no sadness. He offered simple counsel, "Treat me like family." I returned Mr. Harrold to his room, and with a bit of a tremble in my hand, wrote an order in his chart: *Do Not Resuscitate*.

Mr. Harold was seldom alone in the days that followed. Family stayed close at hand, and there were frequent visits from nurses, aides, and the myriad of staff that had come to know the gentle farmer in the corner room. He seemed embarrassed by the attention, but looked at every face with appreciation. He had become too weak to leave his room, even by wheelchair, and sitting up became an ordeal. Our focus changed from diagnosis and cure to comfort and caring. Little did I realize that both approaches could heal.

Early one Sunday morning, just before ending a long night of duty, I was called to Mr. Harrold's bedside. His family was there, as was his nurse and the hospital chaplain. His blood pressure had fallen quite low, and his pulse had become weak and erratic. We looked into each others' eyes for many moments, and I struggled to honor his request for no sadness. With a faint smile he reached for my hand, held it in his own, and in a soft voice he said, "Thank you for helping me die."

"What do you mean?" I asked, with tears that I tried to deny welling up in my eyes.

"I did not start to live until I started to die," he explained. "I've always believed that some things never had to be said. My life has told my family what I feel for them, but I've never said the words. For the first time, I told my son that I love him. I heard him say that he loves me."

He took a long look around the room, his eyes resting for a moment on his wife and son, and then continued. "The most wonderful thing has happened here. I've learned to like being alone. I've learned to listen to the quiet. It has taken all of these years, but I finally figured it out. Score is not kept here on earth."

With a soft "Thank you," he brought my hand to his lips and kissed it, placed it over his heart, and gently fell off to another place.

It was the realization that my feet were cold that brought my awareness back to the scene before me. It had snowed during the night, the first snowfall of the season, and I was drawn to the tree with the bird feeders after leaving the hospital that morning. I stood in the snow, overwhelmed by the beauty of that ordinary tree in the middle of the city. It would be some time before I understood what had happened that morning. I felt an uncomfortable duality. I was both a physician defeated by death and the witness enriched by it. In time, I would come to accept that my greatest triumphs, my greatest leaps in understanding, would rise from apparent failures and the courage to feel.

Sometimes the teacher appears before we are able to understand the lesson. As I turned to leave, the song of the Carolina wren filled the air, and I knew that my teacher would always travel with me.

CHAPTER 2

I Only Have One to Give

A bit of fragrance always clings to the hand that gives you roses.
CHINESE PROVERB

*If you knew what I know about the power of giving, you would
not let a single meal pass without sharing it in some way.*
BUDDHA

Since my earliest recollections of contemplating a career,
I have been drawn by medicine. A son of a chemist, my
left brain developed with a love of the natural sciences and a
wondrous curiosity. But it was a balanced development, the
right brain nurtured by a loving home, where helping others
was reflexive and unconditional. Becoming a doctor always
seemed to be the logical conclusion for a scientist honoring
the tradition of giving.

While my journey did indeed lead to medicine, the impa-
tience of youth helped me select a circuitous, if not a poorly
worn route. Large universities can be an intimidating place,

but the prospect of eleven years of education was overwhelming to me as a college freshman. The fire service offered a shorter road, and, perhaps, a more exciting one.

Although it was many years ago, the day I first stood at the fork in the road and contemplated taking a different path remains vivid in my memories. Sitting in the student union waiting for a calculus exam, I passed the time by reading my hometown newspaper. Our local fire department was recruiting members, with a pressing need for help staffing the community's new ambulance service. While calculus was haunting my early college career, so were doubts that would intrude upon times of study and quiet. Doubt about my ability to care for ill and injured patients, doubts of my academic prowess, and even doubts of my purpose. By week's end I was sitting in the office of the fire chief and had joined my hometown's volunteer fire department.

In the months that followed, my days were spent in lecture halls and chemistry laboratories chasing expectations. It was the night classes learning emergency victim care and weekly drills at the fire station, however, that touched upon my dreams. The training came easy to me, and I quickly became an Emergency Medical Technician. On the ambulance, I found no doubt. I was comfortable with ill and injured patients. I felt purpose.

Our community was a small one and lacked the ability to provide advanced life support. When the opportunity arose to become a paramedic, I seized upon it without a moment's hesitation. Paramedic school excited me like no college course had ever been able to. Theory for tomorrow was gradually supplanted by knowledge for today. What I had planned as three months off from college to become a paramedic became much more. I accepted a full-time position with the department and after six weeks at the fire academy became one of the city's first firefighter-paramedics. While I saw some disappointment in my parents' eyes, I also saw pride. Every time the bell rang, I was in the service of others.

The fire service was good to me. I found close friendship, confronted and overcame fear, and learned how to teach others. I touched, and was touched by, lives in the hours of their greatest need. I also experienced limitation, encountering need that surpassed my ability to help. At times, I wondered if I could do more.

One morning I was mindlessly watching dawn break over the firehouse. I found comfort in the quiet. Hours earlier I had returned from a run that had gone badly. Called to the home of a thirty-six-year-old man with chest pain, we found him sitting in his bedroom surrounded by young children in pajamas, frightened by the commotion that roused them from their sleep. Despite his protestations that he was fine, his wife knew otherwise. He grew silent as he looked deeply into the eyes of each of his children and slumped into unconsciousness.

The cardiac monitor revealed ventricular fibrillation, that dreaded heart pattern that my training, and even television, had taught me was predictive of death. Electrical paddles were placed to his chest and he was shocked into a normal cardiac rhythm. But the success was brief. Within a minute or two he again slipped back into the shadows of death, and once again was shocked into a more stable picture. The pattern would repeat itself endlessly as needles were inserted into veins, medications administered, and protocols followed. I had lost track of the number of times that he was shocked when we realized, horrified, that his children were still in the room watching.

As the eastern sky lightened, I thought about those children and wondered what they would remember about their father. I wondered if this morning had robbed them of good memories. I hardly noticed as the assistant chief sat down next to me on the bench just outside the firehouse. He was a rather cantankerous man, just a year or two shy of his pension. He was suspicious of the newer ways of fire science and ambulances equipped with advanced life support. Seldom at a loss for words and criticism, he sat with me in silence for many minutes.

Placing a weathered hand on my knee, he looked at me and said, "Son, what are you still doing here?"

Glancing at my watch, I was about to comment that it wasn't time to go home yet when he shook his head saying, "No, I don't mean this morning. I mean in this place, in this work. This is all that I have ever known, all that I can do. This is where I can be my best. I've watched you for three years now. You are good, very good. Your way is better than mine. You have a precious gift, but you can use only a small part of it here. I can't even imagine what your best might be."

I sat in stunned silence as he stood up and made his way back into the firehouse. It occurred to me that I hadn't said a word. Over the days that were to come, his words seemed to follow me everywhere. I felt much satisfaction in what I did, but I was haunted by the thought that I could be doing more.

That's the funny thing about a journey. You can never be quite certain where it will lead until it has been traveled. Perhaps our destinations are placed within us when we come into this world, but the way we get there is for us to choose, much like deciding between the shortest route and the scenic route when leaving for vacation. Not many months after that early morning talk with the chief, I was again sitting in the student union waiting for a calculus exam. The irony was not lost on me, nor was the realization that my journey had not changed.

College seemed easier the second time around, certainly easier than getting up every day and going to work. The course work was the same, but the faces that surrounded me each day seemed so much younger and less disciplined than I remembered. Gone was the doubt. Knowing that I was on the right path, I started to enjoy the view. The eleven years of education that it would take to become a doctor seemed less daunting than they once had. Indeed, they passed all too quickly.

The potential for giving in the practice of medicine is limitless, and I have come to appreciate the act of giving as one of the most powerful forces that can shape the human experience. The receipt of a gift or an act of kindness raises one's level of energy. The physiological changes that occur within the body are well documented: heart rate increases, senses become more acute, and blood flow increases to the parts of the brain associated with pleasure. In essence, we feel good when we receive. The same changes can be observed in those that give. It feels good to give.

The power of giving is perhaps most evident among those that witness it. It makes us feel good to watch an act of giving. Watching a handicapped person being helped across a street, someone giving up a place in line to another at the grocery store, somebody shoveling a neighbor's sidewalk—it all makes us feel good. The force is so powerful that merely seeing an image on television or in the newspaper of people helping others makes us feel good, and it sells newspapers.

I have been most touched in my profession not by what I have been able to do for others, but by what I have observed in others. Physicians are invited into the lives of their patients, often with the trust reserved only for the closest of family or the most special of friends. If you take the time, and sometimes the courage, to step into that life and look around for a while, sometimes you leave with an understanding, a morsel of wisdom that might never again cross your path. I believe this is the potential that that aging fire chief spoke about more than twenty-five years ago.

The power of giving is not reserved to those blessed with professions of service. My efforts seem rather frail compared to those I have encountered among my patients. Misty Reginald taught me much about the power of giving.

I have known Misty for almost eight years, since she was thirty. She is outgoing, charming, and well suited for a career in retail sales. Although she is not a frequent visitor to the office, when she does come, it is usually for one of the common maladies that seem to be a product of our stressed and anxious society. Back pain, reflux, and fatigue probably consume a quarter of my schedule. I had always thought of Misty as being happy, or at least not unhappy. I am only now appreciating that there is a profound difference between the two.

On a recent visit, she was truly happy, not what I had anticipated from someone coming in with complaints of abdominal pain. I could only smile when I saw her sitting on the exam table waiting for me. I have learned to trust my emotions when evaluating patients. Happy people tend to make those around them feel happy as well. When you are in close proximity with someone sad, invariably you begin to feel sad yourself. A key diagnostic aid for some personality disorders is how the clinician feels being around the patient. Only a field of energy could have such an effect, something that medical school does not judge very important to the curriculum.

"If I knew belly pain made someone feel so good, I would have recommended it a long time ago, Misty," I said with a smile.

"Oh, I'm just so happy that my brother-in-law went golfing today," she explained.

"I'll be glad to take a day off this week if it will make you feel even better," I joked.

"It's just that he hasn't been golfing in several years, and he used to enjoy it so," she said.

It took some doing, but I was able to direct the conversation away from what the family was doing for vacation and the current little league standings to her abdominal pain. She admitted that she had only come to keep peace in her family, that her mother had diagnosed her with a fatal disease. Placing her hand across the right side of her upper abdomen, she confessed that she had felt discomfort for at least a month. She had thought it would get better on its own, but the burning pain persisted and she was having problems hiding the fact from her friends and family.

Lifting her shirt to take a look at the area, I was jolted with shock. "What has happened to you!" I nearly shouted.

A huge surgical scar, obviously recent, jumped out at me. The telltale railroad-track wound started just right of her midline and stretched around her right side, ending near the middle of her back. It looked as if someone had tried to cut her in half.

"Oh that," she explained matter-of-factly. "I gave my kidney to my brother-in-law. Didn't they send you a report? They said they would."

The surprise was so abrupt that I had to sit down as she told me about her brother-in-law. He had been a diabetic since childhood and had suffered many complications, the most difficult being kidney failure. He was on dialysis for several years, but while the treatments kept his body alive, what it was that made him Tim gradually disappeared. It was ironic. While the machine prolonged life, each treatment was a day lost from life. The four hours on the machine each session was followed by two or three hours of light-headedness and often nausea. Work was usually impossible on treatment days, but he tried hard. All too often, his day ended in frustration and surrender.

His years on dialysis were difficult ones, complicated by multiple infections and blood abnormalities. His blood pressure was difficult to control and a day without a headache was cause for celebration. He had four operations to replace shunts, the device that vascular surgeons create beneath the skin to provide a site for the needles that connected him to the machine. Two of the shunts clotted and failed. One shunt had to be removed because of infection, but only after spilling bacteria into the bloodstream and producing an illness that he scarcely survived.

Shortly after starting him on dialysis, Tim's nephrologist recommended a kidney transplant. It would free him from the machine and restore some normalcy to his life. He would be able to take vacations again; even a long weekend seemed too good a possibility to come true. He was referred to a transplant center and the long evaluation to judge his suitability started. Every organ of his body was examined, including his mind. He was told that some people have profound psychological problems with being the recipient of an organ from somebody who died. He passed the transplant evaluation, and with high hopes, was placed on the transplant list. Unfortunately, his blood type was rare, which dramatically limited the number of organs available to him.

Tim spent two years on the transplant list. Perhaps it was worse than the dialysis he wanted to avoid. He lived with a constant sense of expectation, hesitant to go out to the grocery store for fear that the telephone call he was waiting for would come. But it never came. He would find himself watching the evening news for word of traffic fatalities that could generate a donation, and then lying awake at night wracked with profound guilt for wishing tragedy. One by one, fellow patients at the dialysis clinic would stop coming. They all had received organs before him, and he struggled with bitterness and envy.

Late in Tim's second year on the transplant list, a suitable organ became available. It was the same day that he was admitted to the intensive care unit with a blood infection. The infection rendered him ineligible for the transplant and the organ went to a woman who had only been on the transplant list for several months. He fell into a deep depression and started to contemplate suicide. All his family could do was stand by his side and watch the locomotive speed down the tracks toward them.

During Tim's transplant evaluation, consideration was given to a living donation, in which a suitable candidate would donate a kidney. Such a procedure was fraught with risk to the donor, but each of Tim's siblings, parents, and even aunts and uncles had lined up to be tested. No one matched his needs. Misty had always been fond of Tim. After all, he was the brother of the most important person in her life. She had volunteered to be tested with the rest of the family, but since she was not a blood relative, a match would have been a near impossibility and her offer was politely declined. As Tim languished on the transplant list, sustained but not living, she insisted on being tested. She was a close match, not perfect, but she would make an acceptable donor.

Blood and tissue typing was only the first step in determining whether Misty could donate her kidney to her brother-in-law, though. She met with Tim's transplant surgeon, and was rather surprised that he did not seem very enthusiastic about using her as a donor. It was decided that they would not inform the family, not even Tim, until it was certain that she would be an acceptable candidate. Only then would the family be consulted to help her decide whether she should become a donor. Under the guise of visiting a friend, she was checked into the transplant center for three days of poking, prodding, and imaging. Misty felt bad about the deception, but she did not want to deal with the resistance that she anticipated from her family unless it was absolutely necessary.

During those three days, she had countless blood tests, cardiac stress testing, angiograms, total-body CT scans, a colonoscopy, an upper endoscopy, ultrasounds, pulmonary function testing, and physical examinations. She met with nephrologists, cardiologists, pulmonologists, transplant surgeons, vascular surgeons, and even an endocrinologist. She had lengthy conversations with psychiatrists, psychologists, social workers, financial counselors, and even a priest and a rabbi. She met with transplant recipients, kidney donors, and even the widow of a man who died from complications of his donation. The medical community calls it *informed consent*, no doubt a concept first developed by some lawyer to limit a hospital's liability exposure. Patients and families are deluged with facts and figures and expected to make decisions that physicians often struggle with. But Misty's decision was not to be made with statistics and logic. It was to be made with love.

She had mixed emotions when she met with the transplant surgeon two weeks after her evaluation. Ecstatic that she was accepted as a donor, she dreaded the next step, telling her family. They accepted the news better than she had expected, certainly with surprise and concern for her safety, but also with pride at her generosity and courage. Surprisingly, the only member of the family against her donation was her brother-in-law. He worried about something going wrong, living at her expense, and, perhaps, living in guilt. One night they sat for hours in a field behind his home, watching shooting stars, listening to the whip-poor-will, and gaining wisdom through the silence.

Misty thought about those shooting stars, and the wish she made that night, as she laid on a gurney waiting to be taken into the operating room. She had wished for courage and the ability to see her donation through to the end. She was very frightened and didn't want anyone to know. She would go first, and the operation would take many hours. Tim's operation would start near the conclusion of hers, and would not be as difficult or last as long. She was expected to remain in the hospital for at least a week, while Tim would be home after several days.

Misty's operation went well, but the amount of pain afterwards was more than she had expected. The narcotics she was given robbed her of most memories from the first post-operative days, but some things are best forgotten. Misty's first clear recollection was waking up on the third day after the operation with her brother-in-law sitting in a wheelchair at her side, his face resting on the bed. She could feel the bed shake with his sobs. She had never seen him cry before, and now he seemed inconsolable.

Misty ran her hand through her brother-in-law's hair, stroked his face, and in a soft voice soothed, "It's okay, Tim, I'm doing all right. Everything is going to be just fine."

He looked up at her with an expression that frightened her. Perhaps his grief was not for her. Perhaps something had gone terribly wrong.

Choking back tears, he whispered, "I made urine today. I haven't made urine in two years!"

Then it was her turn to cry, and she fell asleep in his arms.

Misty told me that she had cried a lot since that day. But the tears were different. She had never understood the phrase "tears of joy," but now she found herself living it. All she had to do was to look at her brother-in-law and her eyes would start to well up with happiness and gratitude. In just a few short months his life had been transformed, and he took her along for the ride. He had gained weight, he felt energized, and now he dared to make plans for the future. He had once again become the person that she had known many years before, but there was also something different. When she looked into his eyes she saw a depth that she hadn't noticed before, much like the endless field of stars she saw looking into the night sky. The Tim she had known was on the surface, but there was also a sense that there was so much more of him to learn about, a greatness just below the surface that went on forever.

Most of my days are spent listening. Typically the stories I hear are those from the body; an ache here, a pain there, stories composed by our consciousness and edited by our egos. Every once in a great while I hear a story from the heart. The warmth that wrapped around me like a blanket and the serenity that I felt told me that Misty's was one of those stories. But the depth that I saw in her eyes told me more; it had also been a story from the soul.

It is difficult to go from communicating with the soul to discussing belly pain, but with an office schedule now gravely behind, I reluctantly steered our conversation back to the reason for her visit. Misty's mother subscribed to the principle that "no good deed goes unpunished," and daily voiced her conviction that the pain was something serious caused by the organ donation. Even her husband, an optimistic man by nature, felt an unusual unease that his mother-in-law's gloom helped nourish. Misty herself started to find the words *what if* in her thoughts during the quiet of the night.

"And what if, Misty?" I gently asked.

"Well, that's the whole point," Misty sighed. "It's not about me. At this very minute Tim is playing golf for the first time in years. People that are getting ready to die don't play golf. There is no amount of pain, no diagnosis that you can give me, that will diminish the joy that I feel in knowing that his life is back."

My examination was brief, but there was nothing in the description of her discomfort or in her answers to my questions that gave me much cause for concern. The discomfort was rather superficial and in close proximity to the surgical wound. Most likely it was produced by nerve tissue that was interrupted by the incision, and it would get better over time. The scar too would lighten and become less noticeable over time, but it would always be present to serve as a reminder of her act of kindness. It told a story that few would ever come to know.

I couldn't help but wonder about the many other scars that I had seen, and how many could have told tales of something other than illness and pain, had I looked for them. And I contemplated giving. My experience with giving was limited to time and occasionally money. Misty gave of herself. I once read an article about a spiritual master living in India. He was asked about the meaning of life, and he replied that the purpose of life was to give it away. It wasn't until I saw that scar that I started to understand.

I reassured Misty that her discomfort was nothing to be concerned about, but I had the feeling that I was telling her something that she already knew. She declined medication for pain, insisting that it was there for a reason, and it would pass in its own time. I thanked her for sharing her story with me and observed that hers was a generosity that I seldom encountered in medicine, one that she should be proud of.

Embarrassed, Misty looked down at the floor, slowly shaking her head. She said, "No, the giving was the easy part. Tim had the hard part. I have never had the chance to help someone before. At least, not in an important way. Maybe I just never looked for a way to help someone. Tim gave me that reason to look, and the desire to help. Sometimes, it is harder to accept a gift than it is to give. That was the way it was with Tim and I.

"Since the operation my life has changed. I feel as if I have been cured of depression, but I didn't realize that I had been depressed. I thought I had always been happy, but now I know that what I once thought was happiness was something much less. I have always expected the fine things in life to come tomorrow, but now I know that they are here today. Tim made it possible for me to experience life, and to share his with him. To be honest, I have received much more than anything I have given."

I let her words sink deep inside of me as we sat in silence for a few moments. I felt wisdom far beyond the two of us and knew these moments to be profoundly special. I asked her if she had any regrets. She replied with a smile, "Just one. I only have one to give."

CHAPTER 3

Shot While Escaping

Forgiveness is the fragrance the violet sheds
on the heel that has crushed it.
MARK TWAIN

D octors are often quick to judge. From the initial days
of medical school we are taught to apply the scientific
method and statistical analysis when examining the claims
made about new drugs and better procedures in the medical literature. We can quickly discard some articles as junk
and save those that are worthy of our time for further study.
Learning physical examination comes through repeated determination of *normal* or *abnormal*. Laboratory studies become
swiftly known as *good* and *bad*. We are taught to honor tradition and to be skeptical of new ways.

During residency, judgment skills are honed to a cutting edge. The emergency department is the training ground
for quick clinical decisions. There we learn to distinguish
sick patients from those with less urgent needs, a judgment
that impacts everything that happens to that individual. We

become so good at judging that sometimes it is difficult not to let facts sway us from our preconceived notions.

Quick judgment becomes so routine in the practice of medicine that it is but a small step for the habit to infiltrate personal life. It took me a long time to become a doctor. It has taken even longer to recognize that the skills that serve me well professionally can narrow my vision of life and make me judgmental of the world around me. Once again, my patients have been my teachers.

When I moved from my hometown for residency training, I found myself in a large, strange city, and found that life there was different than what I had known in a small town. Some neighborhoods were more prosperous than others, many people looked different from me, and certain parts of town were considered unsafe. Every morning the local newspaper would detail the violence that had occurred in the streets the night before and hypothesize about the cause of rising crime and corruption. Every morning the newspaper brought fear to my doorstep.

On my commute to work, I would drive through neighborhoods filled with clutter, peeling paint, and rusted automobiles. The closer I got to the hospital, the deeper the decay penetrated. Graffiti spoke a foreign language from every building and wall, and groups of youths hung out on street corners. News radio always made the trip with me and kept me current on the city's homicide rate, making sure that I hadn't missed a single detail in the morning's newspaper. Every morning the radio brought fear to my commute.

In those first years, I was much too busy to give undue attention to the paper and the television. That was probably a good thing, but I would be naïve to believe that they did not contribute to the stress of my new life. The community always seemed to be in conflict. White against black, suburbs against the inner city, and the haves against the have-nots, one group always seemed to be in conflict with another. Every harsh word, every accusation, and every suspicion was recorded by the media and replayed to the community. Often I would wonder whether the media was reporting the news or helping to create it.

One day the city awoke to a sensational story that would capture the headlines and the awareness of the community for weeks. A black man had been shot by a white police officer. Every detail was laid out in the newspaper. Racial tension in the inner city was reportedly dangerously high.

The drama had started when a security guard working for a grocery store had grown suspicious of a man's behavior and begun watching him closely. Apparently the security guard had seen the man slip an object into his coat and walk out of the store. The security guard followed and notified a police officer who happened to be in the parking lot. As the man was getting into his car, the officer yelled for him to stop. The car started to pull away, and the officer reached through the open window, grabbed the steering wheel, and was drug off his feet before letting go. Feeling his life was in danger, the police officer fired three shots through the back window of the car as it started to drive away. Shot in the back, the driver lost control of his car, which jumped a curb and struck a woman and her five-year-old son. By dawn the human cost had started to be tallied—a suspected shoplifter hospitalized with a gunshot wound, a five-year-old boy in the intensive care unit with critical injuries, and a traumatized young police officer.

It was a story that would not end. Dueling press conferences traded charges and counter-charges of police brutality, softness on crime, and racism on a daily basis, all televised live and analyzed on talk radio. Investigations were launched, and the investigators were investigated. Protests and marches became routine. Social advocacy groups decried city hall's support of bad cops, while the police union decried city hall's lack of support. By the time the wildfire died out, the city was polarized. Nobody could be found without an opinion. Nobody could be found with all the facts.

A number of years later, a new patient sat waiting for me in an examination room. His doctor was leaving the area and asked that I assume his care. I knew that he had been injured by a gunshot wound, but it wasn't until I saw his name on the chart that I realized that the Peter Marks that I had promised to see was the same man who had been shot by the police in the shoplifting incident. My medical assistant recorded the reason for his visit on the chart, and I groaned when I saw that he was there for a refill of pain medication. I was immediately suspicious, and I walked into the room with expectations of dislike.

Peter was sitting in a wheelchair with a small frame and solid wheels, of the type popular with paraplegics who like an active lifestyle. He wore fingerless gloves on each hand, no doubt to make moving the chair more comfortable. He slipped off his right glove, extended his hand to me, and said with a smile, "Excuse me for not standing, sir. I'm very happy to meet you."

He was a big man, and probably would have stood well over six feet tall. His upper body was well developed, the muscular definition visible through his T-shirt. His handshake was firm, yet had a gentle quality about it. There was a gentleness in his voice as well, and it seemed to reflect a genuine respect. There was a warmth about him that didn't seem to match the preconceptions that I had developed in the hall. So far, I hadn't seen the monster that I had read about in the newspaper, and I wondered whether I had confused him with another Peter Marks.

As I skimmed through the records that his previous doctor had forwarded, though, there was no doubt that this was indeed the infamous Peter Marks. The extent of his injuries, however, surprised me. It was strange how it had been neglected by the media. The bullet had struck and shattered the tenth thoracic vertebra. He had undergone surgery to stabilize the injury, but the spinal cord was damaged at that level. He was discharged from the hospital after several weeks, but spent the better part of a year in a rehabilitation center learning a new way to live. The damaged spinal cord could not be repaired and he would spend the rest of his life in the wheelchair. He had no sensation below his navel, and needed to worry constantly about injuries to his legs that could go unrecognized and become infected. He was unable to urinate or have a bowel movement spontaneously and was taught to pass a catheter into his bladder four times a day to drain urine. Daily bowel movements could occur only with mechanical stimulation of the rectum. Sexual intimacy, if it occurred at all, would be profoundly different for this thirty-four-year-old man.

Pain would also accompany him into the future. He told me that his medication reduced his pain, but did not take it away. The pain seemed worse when he was more active in his chair, but the thought of spending more time alone in his apartment was considerably more disagreeable. He also didn't want his medication increased, as it made him too tired. He wanted to experience all that life offered him, with a clear and sharp mind, even if part of the experience was pain.

At the end of our first visit, after I had refilled his medications, he paused before leaving and asked, "Doc, why didn't you ask me if I did it?"

"Well," I replied, a little surprised at his forthrightness, "it wouldn't have changed your medical problems, and it isn't any of my business."

He was quiet for a moment, then said, "But I need your help, and you need my honesty. Yes, I stole from the store, but I didn't know that the officer was trying to stop me, and I never would have tried to hurt him. And that child, I can see his face every night in my sleep."

"What did you take, Peter?" I asked.

"It was a bottle of Advil," he replied.

I was dumfounded. "You were shot over a bottle of Advil?" I asked in dismay.

"Well, I guess the cop didn't know that. Anyways, it doesn't make much difference now," he said stoically. "At least they didn't send me to prison. They told me that if I would plead guilty I would only get probation."

"Judging from what I saw on television, the prosecutor didn't seem to be the compassionate type," I commented.

Peter smiled and noted, "I don't think compassion had anything to do with it. It was simple economics. If they had sent me to jail, the county would have had to pay my medical bills." With the wrench of an arm he turned his chair and rolled out of the room.

I saw Peter often. His pain medication was a controlled substance that could not be refilled, requiring a new prescription every month. It was difficult for him to make it across town to my office, but he never complained. I could have arranged for him to be seen at a hospital clinic close to his home, but he wanted to see me. With each visit, I learned a little bit more about this man who had mysteriously appeared in my life.

He was one of six children in his family, the oldest of two boys. His younger brother had died of a drug overdose when they were teenagers. His four sisters, two younger and two older, all had children and lived nearby. The role of favorite uncle had always made him feel special and had been a large part of his life. During his long hospitalization, however, the kids got out of the habit of stopping by his apartment on their way home from school. A couple were even frightened of him, fearful that he had something that they could catch.

Peter and his sisters were raised by a single mother in a two-bedroom apartment in the housing projects, an area of town known for its toughness. He had never known his father; not much had ever been said of him. They had never had much money, never had extras, but somehow, their mother had always made sure that they had enough. What he remembered the most, however, was that they had always felt love. His mother was ill by the time I started to see Peter, and was not expected to live without a liver transplant, an unlikely happening among people of meager means. She lived in a building without an elevator, so Peter couldn't see her very much and trusted her care to the hands of his sisters.

It was hard for him to learn to depend on others. It had taken years living in the projects to learn just the opposite. The need for others when you were growing up in the projects was usually met by one of the numerous gangs, just a stone's throw from drug dealing and prison. But paralysis is a good teacher and tends to quiet the ego. Transferring from the chair to his bed at night was always a high-risk maneuver. A slip found him on the floor without the ability to get up. After spending a number of nights on the floor, he found gratitude for the friends and neighbors in his apartment building who checked on him regularly. They had become family, and like family, he could not live without them.

On one of Peter's office visits, he mentioned that he was waking up at night with chills. He felt a little more tired than usual, but otherwise felt his normal self. Paraplegics are prone to a host of infections, and in fact, infection is often what they die from. Even a first-year medical student would hear *chills* and think *infection*. I examined him carefully that day, but couldn't find anything of concern. Urinalysis didn't suggest a urinary tract infection, a common problem in paraplegics who require catheterization. To be thorough, I drew blood before sending him on his way for another month, but I felt reasonably certain that he was doing well.

My optimism deflated as quickly as a balloon the next day when his laboratory work came back. Not that anything was markedly abnormal; his white blood cell count was only slightly elevated, but there were subtle changes that suggested something was amiss. I was concerned about the possibility of infection and the difficulty of locating it in a man with no sensation in most of his body. I arranged for urine and blood cultures, and scheduled a chest X-ray and CT scan of his abdomen and pelvis.

A number of days later, I stood with a radiologist in a dark room gazing into a light box that held Peter's X-ray studies. No bacteria had grown from his blood or urine, so I was hoping that the answers would be found in front of us. In a way, I was hoping that the answers were not there. We couldn't find anything abnormal on the chest X-ray. Even the CT scan looked good. We were looking for an abscess or a deep-seated infection that could explain his chills and presumed fevers, but it wasn't to be found on the study. Before putting the films away, I wanted to see if I could see his original injury, curious if the severity of the injury was still evident. I do not see many CT scans in the course of a day, and I struggled to find the tenth thoracic vertebra. It just didn't seem to be there. The radiologist had difficulty finding it as well. In fact, several of the vertebrae in that area appeared obscure.

Peter was brought back to the hospital for a special scan of his back. Several vertebrae in the central spine were extensively eroded, essentially eaten away by some process. The tenth thoracic vertebra was almost gone. Most likely we had found the source of his symptoms, and it was not good. As I looked at the scan, I flashed back to my medical school days of memorizing the possible causes of such destruction—bacterial infection, tumor, TB of the spine. The cause was now a secondary issue; it would be identified in due course. The immediate concern was for the stability of his spine. A transfer to bed, lifting an object, or even wheeling his chair, Peter was an inopportune movement away from the collapse of his spine and catastrophe.

The neurosurgeons were called and Peter was placed in bed wearing a back brace. The next day found Peter in the operating room. It was indeed an infectious process, and once the destroyed tissue had been cleaned away and sent to the laboratory for cultures, the surgeons set about providing support to his back that his spine could no longer offer on its own. It was a difficult operation, requiring over eight hours. Two titanium rods were placed alongside his backbone, secured with screws, nuts, and bolts—a solution that a mechanic would have been proud of. He would have limited movement of his back and his activities would likely be further reduced, but it was a solution that offered him the ability to get back into his chair and some level of independence. It didn't seem much to offer, but Peter was thrilled, finding blessings in any future that would not confine him to bed.

The cultures from his back grew *Staphylococcus*, and as bad as a staph infection is, this one was worse. The bacteria were resistant to all but the most powerful of antibiotics available. Peter would require six weeks of intravenous antibiotics, much of it in the hospital, and extensive rehabilitation. During the entire process, I didn't hear Peter complain once. Well, there was that time when his dinner tray was delivered; the hospital pathologist couldn't have identified what lay on that plate.

Shortly after Peter's operation, I was sitting in the nursing station writing a note and overheard a conversation between a young physical therapist and her supervisor. The therapist didn't want to take care of Peter. She had heard all about him. Her boss was unsympathetic and told her that she did not have a choice. She didn't have to like him, just take care of him. Then she offered her young charge a bit of advice. On each visit she should take satisfaction in knowing that he had received what he deserved, that death would have been too easy. I'm not sure I had ever encountered such insensitivity before, or at least insensitivity so freely offered, so openly displayed. I felt angry, but I also felt sorry for both of them.

I remained silent, but I took a personal interest in Peter's physical therapy progress. I would linger outside his door during his sessions and often conveniently drop by his room when I knew the therapist was working with him. He was always hard at work, and never seemed to need her pushing in order to reach the next goal. Every word he spoke to her showed respect and gratitude, even during painful maneuvers. She was young enough to be his daughter, but he addressed her as *ma'am* and *miss*. As the days turned into weeks, I noticed that she seemed to spend longer with Peter than her other patients. Her progress notes became less curt. *The subject* gradually became *Mr. Marks*, and eventually *Peter*. On more than one occasion I saw her slip into his room with a bag of fast food. Peter wasn't the only one healed during those weeks.

It would be several months before I would see Peter back in the office. From the hospital he was transferred to the rehabilitation center, where every day was hard work, but Peter told me that it was the kind of hard work that made you feel good. He was back at his apartment and had started volunteering his time as the local Boys' Club after school. He figured that he had the time that most people didn't, and maybe he could keep some kids off the street. His back was a little more stiff than it used to be, but he enjoyed shooting hoops with the boys, and every once in a while, he forgot that he was in a wheelchair.

But we had a new challenge to deal with. During his hospitalization and rehabilitation he developed bed sores from the immobility and the length of time that he was confined to bed. Initially the size of a dime, the ulcers over his sacral region enlarged and deepened. Despite daily cleaning and dressing changes, the wounds grew progressively larger and deeper. The surgeons debrided the ulcers—a nice clean term for cutting away dead and dying tissue to allow the wounds to heal. Like the disease itself, the cure left his wounds even larger and deeper. But healing was elusive, and the cycle of deepening wounds and surgical debridement would repeat itself every few weeks.

As the months passed, Peter spent more and more time in the hospital with wound infections. Cultures revealed the same staph species that had infected his spine, but over time the bacteria learned new tricks and became resistant to our antibiotics. Often the bacteria spilled into Peter's blood stream, leaving him gravely ill and requiring weeks of progressively stronger antibiotics that had to be given intravenously. Eventually, the infection became resistant to all antibiotics. He was fitted with a special pump that would provide a continuous flow of antibiotics into his bloodstream. The antibiotics could not clear the infection, but they might perhaps suppress it. Eventually, the infection would no longer be contained even through these heroic efforts.

As sick as Peter became, he never surrendered to displays of anger or doubt. Instead, he focused on others, eagerly discussing his plans to return to the Boys' Club and working with his kids. Somehow, he always seemed to get better, and always returned to the kids.

One morning my office routine was interrupted by a call from Peter. He wanted to be seen, and on finding that we had no openings, asked if I would add him on to the end of the day. It was a day when the treadmill seemed to be running at an unusually brisk pace and I had multiple hospitals to visit after office hours, but it occurred to me that Peter had never asked me for a favor. You would have thought that I had given him a thousand dollars when he learned that I would see him rather than going to lunch. By the time my last patient of the morning had left, Peter was waiting patiently in the waiting room with a bucket of fried chicken and all of the trimmings. But nobody would be eating chicken that day.

As I led him to an examination room, I knew something was very wrong. I saw fear in his eyes, something that I had never seen before. Considering everything that he had gone through with stoicism and daring, the contemplation of something that Peter would find frightening was frightening in itself. Without saying a word, he reached out and placed a small object in my hand. Turning it over in my hand, I looked at what appeared to be a three-quarter-inch stainless steel nut with confusion.

"Where did this come from, Peter?" I asked.

In a hushed whisper he replied, "It fell out of me."

Certain that I had misunderstood, I asked, "What do you mean it fell out of you?"

"I was changing my dressings this morning," he explained, "and when I reached up inside of me, this fell into my hand. What does it mean?"

It was hard to imagine how a metal nut could find its way into a wound, unless it had happened during a dressing change, but that, too, was difficult to picture. We struggled to get Peter up on the examination table and onto his side so that I could examine him. I removed the bandages and voluminous dressings that covered his lower back and sacrum, and could only stare in disbelief. Much of Peter—his upper buttocks and lower back—was gone. My thoughts flashed back to my days spent in the gross anatomy laboratory in medical school. The sight before me could have been one of those partially dissected cadavers. As my gloved hand and much of my forearm disappeared into the wound, my medical assistant had to leave the room, feeling faint and ill. I didn't feel too well myself.

Exposed bone could easily be seen and much of his pelvis could be felt along the floor of the cavernous wound. The wound tunneled up his back and around his spine. Two large steel rods could be seen protruding from this mass of tissue, no doubt the hardware placed years earlier to stabilize his spine. The end of each rod was threaded. One held a nut, the other didn't.

While Peter was helped to dress and get back into his wheelchair, I placed a call to his surgeon and infectious disease doctor. Neither seemed too surprised by the news, as the battle had long been one of delay. No longer contained by the antibiotics, the infection was consuming flesh and tissue at an alarming rate, and would eventually claim Peter's life. There was nothing left to offer Peter, except perhaps the caring environment of hospice, where the terminally ill can find both physical and emotional comfort as they complete their journeys.

I sat in the sanctuary of my office for a few minutes before joining Peter. The photographs of birds on the walls, the soft music, and the comfortable chair brought little of the peace they were intended to produce. I had never found it easy to tell people bad news, but at least I could find some comfort in understanding the reasons behind it. I could find no understanding of Peter's journey these past years. "All over a bottle of Advil," I said quietly to myself as I turned that surgical nut over and over in my hand.

There was nothing I could say to Peter that he hadn't already known or suspected. I have found that reality is unlikely to produce anything as horrible as what we can imagine. Even the worst of news often comes with some element of relief. Such was the case with Peter. While he certainly didn't show elation at the news, there also wasn't the shock and anger that I had come to expect in such situations. If anything, he appeared almost peaceful.

I let him sit in quiet contemplation for a number of minutes before asking him, "What are you thinking, Peter?"

"Well," he said, "I've been worrying that one day you were going to tell me that the infection was back, that it couldn't be treated, and that it was going to kill me."

"Peter, I'm so very sorry, but that is what I told you," I said hoping that the softness of my voice could temper the harshness of my message.

"Exactly," he reassured me. "Now I don't have to waste another minute of my life worrying about something that I have no control over."

It was not the first time that the wisdom of his words had touched me deeply. He had once seemed such an unlikely source of wisdom to me, a disabled man from the inner city, but now our differences seemed to make him all the more special. Peter hadn't changed any, but I certainly had.

"Peter," I said shaking my head, "you're simply amazing. I knew from that first visit that you were a special person."

"Because you were expecting an angry black man?" he teased.

"Well, yes. Most people would have been consumed by anger over what has happened, and continues to happen, to you. And yet I have never seen you mad."

"I was angry once. When I was in the hospital after being shot, I would lie in bed and cheer the rioting and looting I saw on the TV. I felt such hatred that I wanted to become everything that the newspapers wrote about me." Looking uncharacteristically uncomfortable, he looked down at the floor and continued, "I never told anyone this, mainly because I do not want to remember myself that way."

"What happened? What brought about such a change?" I asked.

Peter looked at me as if the answer was too simple for words. "I forgave them," he said.

"I forgave all of them—the cop, the suits, the prosecutor, the reporters, all of them. One day I heard my nephew say that he was going to join the gang in his neighborhood and help them get even for what happened to me. I was shocked that such hatred could be heard in the voice of a small boy, but when that boy is your nephew it becomes very personal. This loving child was taught to hate, by me. I never realized how angry I had become, and how that anger could spread to others until that day. In that very instant, like someone turning on a light in a dark room, everything my mother had tried to teach me suddenly made sense. I held that boy in my arms as if I was protecting him from wild animals, wild animals that I had set loose. I wanted him to feel nothing but love, but I didn't have very much of that in my body to give. I became aware of an overwhelming desire to forgive, and in the process, I felt peace that I hadn't known before, almost like I was the one who was forgiven."

The fear that I had seen in his eyes earlier was gone, replaced with just a hint of a tear, but it was not a tear of sadness. It was the same tear that you sometimes see when someone receives a precious gift. Peter reached for my hand while concluding, "I haven't felt anger since that day. I have not a single regret." He shook my hand slowly, lingering for a few moments with my hand firmly enveloped by his as those eyes peered into mine. Without another word, he rolled out the door and out of my life.

I sat in stunned silence. As a physician, I've heard many stories, from all types of people, from all walks of life. On rare occasions, I am trusted, and blessed, with a story from the heart. Like Peter, the story was special. It was one of those stories from the soul, that part of us not concerned with death, but with how we go about experiencing life. But a busy office does not lend itself to such contemplation. It would not be until evening that I could find the quiet to sit and reflect upon Peter.

Over the years, I had always seen Peter's as a life that had been profoundly changed. But it wasn't the bullet that changed it. Although horrific, that was merely a challenge among countless others that the human experience must navigate. It provided one of those forks in the road that we get to choose between, opportunities to learn, potential to grow. It was the act of forgiveness that changed Peter's life. Seldom have I encountered a more profound illustration of the power of forgiveness, power that exerts its greatest effects upon those that forgive, rather than those forgiven. Without forgiveness, the past steals from the present moment and our ability to grow and achieve the greatness that lies within each of us.

Peter was not the only one changed by the power of his forgiveness. The lives that he touched will carry that energy with them on their own journeys, be they those of a physical therapist, a youth from the streets, or a tired doctor. It was energy with infinite potential, flowing constantly outward as those forgiven learned how to forgive others. The forgiving life has great vision, able to see not only transgressions, but the energy patterns among our lives that nourish and propagate them. We choose the energy that we journey through and make a part of our lives. The books we read, the movies we watch, and even the conversations in which we participate all contribute to our energy states. As for me, fear is no longer delivered to my doorstep, and with the click of a switch, it no longer accompanies me on my drive to work.

CHAPTER 4

Life Is What You Think It Is

*I went to the woods because I wanted to live deliberately,
to front only the essential facts of life, and see if I could not
learn what it had to teach, and not, when I came to die,
discover that I had not lived.*
HENRY DAVID THOREAU

Much like the lengthening shadows cast by the late-day sun, medicine has thrown its influence over most of my journey in this life. It has come with the satisfaction of service, the challenge of mastery, and the thrill of discovery. I once found those discoveries in the pages of journals and the tedium of conferences, but I now find them in the people that I encounter every day. Many are new to me, many I will never see again, but many more have become familiar companions on my journey. I have found something to learn from all.

Every once in a while, we encounter people who are truly special. Their mere presence makes us feel better, and judging by those that gather around them at parties and gatherings, others feel good in their presence as well. Of course, the opposite is also true. Some people evoke feelings of irritation and depression in others without the exchange of a single word, and they often find themselves alone and isolated. The field of their energy alone seems to effect such power and influence on others.

Energy fields do not come up very often in medical school, and traditional medicine finds comfort only in that that can be seen, touched, and easily measured. Understanding and manipulating fields of energy, however, is at the foundation of many practices in Eastern medicine. Acupuncture, healing touch, and energy medicine are but a few of the myriad techniques that purport to interact with the energy fields of the body to help effect healing. It is hard for the ego of the Western-trained physician to accept that healing could occur without medical or surgical intervention.

Western physicians have no difficulty recognizing the importance of electrical energy in the maintenance and regulation of life itself, however. Our definition of death incorporates the absence of electrical activity within the heart and brain. Electrical changes can be measured at the cellular level. The electrocardiogram measures the electrical activity across the surface of the heart, the electroencephalogram the electrical activity within the brain, and the electromyelogram measures the electrical activity produced by muscle. Elementary physics teaches us that electrical charges and current produce fields of electromagnetic energy, as anyone who lives near high-voltage transmission lines routinely experiences. It seems such a small step, an intellectual chip shot, to move from the acceptance of forces of energy that act within the body to fields of energy that extend from the body.

I believe these special people we encounter have particularly strong life forces, sustained by levels of energy so high that they are able to elevate the energy levels of those around them. Erin was one of those people.

I met Erin on my first day of private practice. Just hours from residency, I was confident in my abilities to manage the sickest of the sick. I could quote landmark articles from a host of medical journals. I could make complicated acid-base calculations and act upon the results. I could perform countless procedures, and if need be, keep a table alive in the ICU overnight. But I didn't have the slightest idea about caring for a sore throat, a rash, or indigestion. I had spent three years perfecting skills that would help me deal with a mere 5 percent of medical problems. Standing outside of the closed examination room door that sheltered me from my first patient, I realized that I was about to start learning the other 95 percent of medicine.

Erin had started working for the large group practice that I had joined not long after becoming a nurse. It did not take long to realize why every doc in the practice wanted to work with Erin. Her skills as a nurse were exceptional, second only to her skills in dealing with people. Many people can be difficult to work with in a medical practice, with physicians frequently at the top of the list. As all of the physicians in the practice were on the faculty at the nearby medical school, strong personalities and fragile egos added to the challenge. Erin managed all, without anyone realizing that they had been managed. Having Erin assigned to work with me was more than good fortune, it changed my expectations about medicine and about myself.

She was incredible with patients, most likely because to her, they were not patients but friends. Something about Erin had a calming effect on people, quite an asset in a medical office. People felt better after being in her presence. It was not uncommon for patients' complaints to have diminished by the time I walked into the exam room. Invariably, they had spent time with Erin.

In those early years she taught me a lot about medicine. As patients arrived at the office, their vital signs would be jotted on a note clipped to the chart, along with her perception of why they came. Part of the challenge of patient care, and part of the stress during those initial days in practice, was figuring out just why somebody had come to the office. Stated reasons, or the infamous "chief complaint," seldom told the whole story, or even the important story. I learned to trust her insight, mainly because she was always right about people. For the most part, medicine is a rather simple job. If you ask the right questions, most people will tell you what is wrong with them. But Erin helped me see that asking the right question wasn't enough. You had to be willing to listen for the right answer.

Academic practice brought with it a steady stream of patients, vast resources from colleagues, and even some stature in the community. It was a safe harbor from which to tailor the knowledge of medicine into the practice of medicine. But I longed for a practice of my own, to find the bond with people that in my youth I had hoped medicine would bring, a bond that Erin had demonstrated was possible. After three years, I left the group to start a practice in the neighborhood where I lived. I was deeply touched and thrilled that Erin wanted to move with me, as she could have had her choice of working with any physician in the city. But I was also a little worried. Starting a new practice was fraught with risk, risk that I could accept for myself, but Erin was leaving the security of a good job.

Starting the new practice brought adventure, excitement, and great satisfaction, and as expected, Erin was central to all of it. I was never quite sure if patients were coming to see me, or Erin. Scores of patients followed us from the old practice, and with them came their families and friends, providing a healthy patient base on which to grow. I was joined in practice by a physician fresh out of residency, and just as she had done for me years earlier, Erin helped him learn that medicine was less about knowing the right answer as it was appreciating the journey that we embarked upon through the lives of our patients. It was fun to watch his transition from that of a good doctor to a caring physician.

As the practice grew outward, its staff grew inward. We became family. Erin was the mother and made it her business to take care of everyone. Coffee was always ready in the morning, our lunches analyzed for proper nutritional value, and our schedules protected to allow time for the other important things in life. The troubles of one became the troubles of all, and good fortune felt by one was relished by all. Erin's two daughters became a fixture in the office after school, able to exploit a vast resource of interests and talent to complete homework assignments and school projects. We watched them grow up and felt pride in their accomplishments.

If our staff was family, then our patients became our extended family. Erin looked after them as well. She was particularly gifted with the elderly. She would note important dates in the lives of our patients on her calendar, and would call at the appropriate time to let them know that somebody cared. Those who did not drive she would pick up on her way to work and drive home again during her break. She worried about our older patients who lived alone, and started a system where they would call the office at a certain time every day. If we failed to hear from someone, Erin would be on the telephone to find out why. On weekends she would make these calls from home. One night I ran into Erin at the grocery store. She was embarrassed to be caught shopping for one of our patients—the denture cream gave her away. Although she denied it, I was pretty sure she paid for the groceries herself.

Erin's vocabulary didn't include the word *no*. She was an easy mark when a child came to the door selling something. Fundraisers knew her by name. Stray animals could always find a home. She was the go-to person for any important task, and any task that others didn't want, or wouldn't take. Erin was the frequent topic of many of our family discussions, and she was often chastised for being easily taken advantage of. But her desire to say yes never seemed to be something that she gave much thought to. It was a philosophy of life and a reflection of the soul within.

The more Erin said yes, the more she gave, the more she seemed to attract into her life. Most would call it luck, but if it was, it was incredible luck. Every month or two she would hear a call-in contest on the radio at work, call in, and win. Entering sweepstakes was a hobby, a very successful hobby. But the best example came during a family vacation to Los Angeles. While touring the television studios, Erin was selected out of a game show audience to be a contestant. On national television, she became the grand-prize winner. Was it luck, or something more? Whatever it was, it just seemed to be right.

We all lived the lives of our patients, but Erin did so more deeply than the rest of us, experiencing tremendous highs with their good fortune, and deep pain when medicine could not provide the answers. One patient in particular seemed to touch Erin like none other, reaching down to the depths of her soul with questions that had no answers, and hurt that found little comfort.

Susan Webb was a thirty-year-old lady from southern Georgia who heard about us through a friend of one of our patients. We all fell in love with her gentle personality and Southern drawl. Erin and Susan seemed to bond instantly, and by the time she left the office that first time, you would have thought that they had been lifelong friends. Susan had been seen by two dermatologists for itching, but the medicine they had given her was not helping. In fact, the itching had grown worse. It had become constant and she felt it all over her body. She was finding it difficult to sleep and to concentrate on daily activities.

I spent a lot of time with Susan on that fist visit, but couldn't find any cause for concern in her history or on physical examination. We drew some blood to look for some obscure causes of itching and sent her out with yet a third medication, hoping that my guess would be better than those before me. The new medication brought little relief and the solitary abnormality on the laboratory results made the obscure seem frighteningly plausible. Susan would get a chest X-ray and return to the office for a follow-up visit.

The chest X-ray revealed a large mass, about the size of a softball. While it would take a biopsy to be certain, it seemed likely that the mass, and the cause of the itching, was lymphoma. When patients are asked to come to the office to discuss study results, invariably they anticipate horrible news. But it is hard to transform something as innocent as itching into a life-altering event, and Susan was unprepared to contemplate the possibility of cancer. Erin was devastated by the news.

I had never seen Erin as disturbed as she was over Susan. It seemed more than sadness and concern, it seemed almost personal, as if she had been chilled by the close encounter with mortality. Working for the faculty practice, Erin had spent a lot of time with the oncologists. She had seen many people with cancer. I asked her what was different with Susan.

"Just look at her." Erin replied, surprised that I had not noticed the similarity between them. "Every time I look at Susan, I see myself looking back. We are both the same age, have six-year-old daughters, enjoy the same things, we even dress alike. I could never handle something like this.

"The worst part," Erin added, "is knowing what they are going to do to her and pretending to Susan that it is something that I would do. I've just taken care of too many cancer patients to be one."

Erin never shared the pain that she felt with Susan, and with her typical smile, walked the difficult days of surgery and chemotherapy with her. The treatment made them both ill, but only Susan's symptoms could be seen. It took a couple of years, but eventually, the treatments ended, and Susan was proclaimed to be in remission. I saw her not long ago. Over a decade has passed since her diagnosis, and she enjoys a good life. She has even had another child since those dark days. Looking back, I realize that the special friendship she shared with Erin was as powerful as the surgeon's knife and as potent as the chemotherapy.

I have never been keen about treating family members, concerned that close relationships can cloud professional judgment, but I have been known to relent for simple problems. Such was the case with my office family. One day Erin came to the office with a tender and inflamed ear after wearing a new pair of earrings for several days. What had started as an allergic reaction became infected, a rather simple problem to treat. As expected, her ear got better on antibiotics. A couple of weeks later, Erin noticed a lump behind her ear. The lump was most likely a lymph node that had enlarged in response to her ear infection, and I suggested that we watch it for a while. Remembering my rule about treating family, I sent Erin to an ear, nose, and throat specialist when the lump was still there two weeks later. The ENT doc reassured her that the lump was a lymph node swollen from the infection and placed her on another course of antibiotics.

The entire office started to get concerned when the lump behind Erin's right ear had not changed after another month. Although Erin's ENT doc felt certain of his diagnosis, he put a needle into the lump, probably to reassure all of us. The cytology came back as reactive lymphocytes, exactly what you would expect from a lymph node reacting to an infection. We would have little time for relief, however. After the needle biopsy, the lump started to enlarge, almost doubling its size in a few short weeks. If it was a lymph node, then it was quite angry at being stuck by that needle.

ENT scheduled an open biopsy of the lymph node. It was a minor operation, and Erin was not too concerned about it. She was looking forward to getting rid of it. On the morning that Erin had her biopsy, I was seeing our patients on my rounds in the hospital when I was surprised by a page to pathology. As I dialed the number, I reasoned that the call couldn't be about Erin, as the biopsy would take a couple of days to process. The pathologist told me that the surgeon had requested a frozen section during the procedure, as something did not look quite right. It was a technique that allowed a quick microscopic look at a tissue sample, and sometimes it could provide a preliminary diagnosis.

After a deep breath and a long pause, I heard the voice say, "Your nurse has anaplastic carcinoma of the parotid gland." Erin had cancer.

I have no idea how long I sat there holding that telephone without anyone on the other end. Five minutes? Ten? Time stood still. Questions flooded my consciousness, questions that I had heard many times before, but had never dreamed that I would ever ask. Could there be some mistake? Was it the wrong patient? Should we get another opinion? A page from the operating room brought my thoughts back to reality, but it wasn't a good reality.

The surgeon told me that Erin had suspected that the news was going to be bad. Before going into the operating room, she told him that if he found cancer, he was to close her up and do no more. She was going to require extensive surgery, surgery that would sacrifice the facial nerve and leave her with permanent paralysis and disfigurement. It was surgery that he did not think she would agree to, but without which she would be unlikely to live another year. It was surgery that he wanted me to talk her into.

The days that followed were dark ones. The schedule was filled with patients, but not purpose. The work day brought distraction, but not meaning. The nights were the most cruel of all, leaving us alone with our thoughts and questions why. But the answers were not forthcoming, and peace was not going to come through understanding.

The science of medicine couldn't help us understand why this had happened to Erin, but it offered us some comfort in knowing where to go to learn what to do about it. Erin had an intuitive awareness that she should not have surgery, and while this was the accepted treatment for parotid cancer, I've always had a deep respect for such intuition, even if I didn't know why. The final biopsy report revealed a very rare type of tumor. My partner and I set out to scour the medical literature for guidance. What little there was to find brought no comfort. Erin's tumor type had been described only five other times. It was a particularly aggressive form of parotid cancer. Each of the five cases had been treated surgically, and each patient was dead within a year. Chemotherapy offered little chance of a cure, the literature estimating only a 5 percent five-year survival rate. Only radiation therapy held a glimmer of hope.

Several academic medical centers had been experimenting with a special kind of radiation for parotid cancer, with results vastly superior to those obtained by traditional radiation therapy. Unfortunately it had only been used with patients whose tumors had recurred following surgical treatment, and never with the tumor type Erin had. Being the first in line is never a comfortable place to be in medicine. Her decision would have to be made without the benefit of knowing how others had fared.

During those days of decision and contemplation, we tried to protect Erin by keeping her out of the office, but it was the one place that she seemed to most want to be. I watched in amazement as she consoled those who grieved for her, finding comfort in making others feel less troubled. Life seemed cruel at that moment. How could someone so special carry such a burden? One evening, after everyone had left the office, Erin stopped by to talk. She was having trouble making a decision and wanted some advice.

We talked for a couple of hours. We even laughed about the old days. When I realized that I could look at Erin without tears welling up in my eyes, I knew that she had really come for me. That night we both found acceptance. Understanding would have to come later.

Erin had decided on the neutron beam radiation. She had spent many days examining her life and agonizing over her decision, when she realized that the answer was actually quite simple. When sitting alone in the quiet of the night, long after her family had gone to bed, she found that she could still hear that inner voice that had always been a source of guidance. The most important thing in her life was her family, and her most important work was raising her daughters. She wanted to live long enough to see them out of school. I silently did the math and considered the statistics. How could such a modest goal seem too far to reach?

Erin traveled to Seattle for treatments. Most of the six weeks that she was there, she spent alone, but found comfort in knowing that her family would be spared much of the difficulty that she knew awaited her with the radiation. She called us at the office almost every day, but it would not be until after her return that we would learn just how difficult her days had been. The radiation caused severe burns to her face and neck and inflamed the tissues of her mouth and throat. Eating was difficult at its best. Her gums bled freely with every chew. She lived on milkshakes, but still lost weight rapidly. Nausea and fatigue became the norm and fear was a constant companion, an acquaintance that she would not share with others.

She returned exhausted, but still wearing a smile that made everyone near her smile as well. Her CT scans offered optimism. The tumor was no longer visible. After a month of rest, she would begin chemotherapy designed to protect the gains she had made with radiation. The chemotherapy would claim her hair, leave her ill, and drop her blood counts, making her weak and prone to infections. Feelings of illness would gradually be replaced by anticipation of the next round of chemotherapy, always a week or two away. And so a year would pass, very much in a fog, but like an early spring morning, the haze that always hung just overhead was gradually burned away by the sun and brilliant blue sky was revealed.

While the years that followed would be plagued with complications from her treatment—hearing loss, no saliva, dry eyes, difficulty swallowing, unending dental problems, and thick, leathery skin—Erin treated them all with amused indifference, for she was disease-free. Her oncologist likened the outcome to that of winning the lottery. She had won the game show of life.

Erin returned to work, but volunteered an increasing amount of her life to others. Through a cancer support group, she helped others deal with the seemingly impossible. She taught disadvantaged children how to read. She visited shut-ins. But mostly, she was a mom. There was never a missed soccer game, a bake sale without her special cookies, or a school fundraiser without an organizer. She lived her life, and she enjoyed being a part of the lives of her children and those who had found a place in her heart. She grasped that part of life that most are too busy to reach for. She had returned to a simple life and found abundance. While I had always known Erin to be happy, those years displayed happiness as a part of the infinite—the limitless peace and joy that one finds deep within the soul.

After six years of cancer-free life, Erin began experiencing headaches. Mild and easy to ignore at first, with each passing week they intruded deeper into the happiness that she had found. The oncologist confirmed what all had feared but dared not think. The tumor was back and hard at work. It had eaten deep into the bones of her face and skull, and Erin would require the surgery that she was once desperate to avoid. She lost much of the right side of her face to the surgeon's knife, a loss made less apparent through a series of reconstructive operations. When not awaiting surgery, she was receiving chemotherapy. The passage of time, and of life, was marked by cycles of chemotherapy, the chemicals becoming progressively more toxic as the desperation of her oncologists grew. CT scans and MRIs would search for good news after each cycle of chemotherapy was completed, but they only brought disappointment and more chemotherapy.

While visiting hospital patients one lunch hour, I ran into Erin's oncologist. He told me that she had received chemotherapy the day before and was having relentless nausea and vomiting that could not be controlled. She was in terrible pain, but refused his efforts to give her more pain medication. The medication made her drowsy and often she wouldn't take any of it if she had something important to do that day.

"What could possibly be more important than Erin taking her pain medications?" the oncologist sighed in frustration.

When I returned to the office, there sat Erin, waiting with an elderly lady she had befriended through the years. She lived alone and hadn't been feeling well, but did not have a way to get to the doctor. Days earlier, Erin had insisted on making her an appointment and taking her. As my widowed patient sat with Erin, she realized that she was feeling better. Strangely, the arthritis pain that had occupied her thoughts for many days was difficult to remember. She felt more energetic, and as the two passed the time in conversation, she started to think about that flower bed that needed attention. Erin's smile never once left her face, and with it flowed a warmth that even chemotherapy could not chill. Even knowing how ill Erin was, I too, felt my spirits soar, and was glad she had come.

As Erin cooked dinner and cleaned house, tutored children, and gave precious time to others, her cancer learned new ways to challenge her. Every week or two a small piece of her ear, now possessed with malignant cells, would flake off and fall away. She saw some humor in every look in the mirror, as more often than not, what looked back had changed from the day before. One day a tooth fell from her mouth, the socket weakened by cancer and chemotherapy. Not to be deprived of what meager service it offered her, Erin went to the hardware store, bought some superglue, and glued the molar back in place. A drooping eyelid, changes in vision, and eyes that would not move where she intended mapped the progression of one invaded cranial nerve after another.

Shortly after she was told that the oncologist didn't have anything else to offer, Erin came to see me, this time as a patient. I had known Erin as an employee, a colleague, and as a friend. This would be my least favorite role, an uncomfortable one. Perhaps it was the role through which I was to understand Erin and myself the most. I felt that I had so little to offer. I couldn't cure. I couldn't prolong. I couldn't even keep her out of pain. But Erin was looking for none of these things. She wasn't trying to avoid the journey, she wanted to understand it and learn from it.

When Erin came to see me, she scheduled the last appointment of the day so that we would have time to talk. She knew that I hated to run behind and didn't want me to feel rushed. It had been seven years since she had worked for me, and she was still looking after my schedule. We chatted for a few minutes about family and vacation plans, something that typically puts patients at ease when feeling uncomfortable. But this wasn't any ordinary patient, this was Erin. I looked her in the eyes for many moments, and she looked into mine. I could feel her thoughts. I knew what she wanted, but in a hushed voice I asked the question anyway. "What can I do for you, Erin, how can I help you?"

The smile that was Erin never wavered, the eyes didn't look away for a second, and the succinctness of her request reflected peace and an uncommon understanding of life. "Don't prolong the inevitable. Let me live the experience," she said.

"I've learned so much in the past ten years, and I know that there is much more to learn, perhaps the most important lessons of all," Erin went on. "The oncologists won't let you die and want you to be numb with medications along the way; alive, yet unaware that you live. I'm sure it's easier for them, and heaven knows, it would be much easier that way for my family. The only thing unnatural about death is how we try to defeat it, and when we can't, how we try to hide it."

I was struck by her words and their sincerity. I was even more struck by what I didn't hear—fear, anger, anxiety— everything that I had grown accustomed to dealing with when confronting death with patients. Instead, I heard a voice that unquestionably came from a place of knowledge. It was a place that I wanted to know more about.

"What have you learned, Erin?"

"That life is what you think it is," Erin replied without hesitation. "That you can deal with any challenge, and only then will you find the opportunity to grow and become better. That you do not live until you take a risk at living." She paused in a moment of reflection and continued, "And perhaps most of all, you find the greatest meaning, the greatest happiness, in returning to the basics, surrounding yourself with just the essential parts of life. For me, that was my girls."

My thoughts drifted back to that evening, shortly after her diagnosis, when she shared with me her life goal. Indeed, she had lived to see her daughters raised. In fact, those days vanquished all traces of cancer from her body. As she found those essential ingredients of life, and embraced them, Erin had found healing. I had always equated healing with cure, no doubt the influence of my traditional training, but sitting there with Erin I started to realize that there was a profound difference between the two. True, her cancer returned and eventually would claim her life, but she was much more than a patient with cancer. She was one who observed the patient with cancer, dealing with years of treatment and therapy, and learning from it. She was that energy that touched and lightened the souls of others. She was one who found wealth through giving. She was the focus of divine love that had raised her daughters.

She was the spirit that touched my heart and opened my mind to new possibilities. For me, medicine would never be the same.

CHAPTER 5

Retire While You Are Still Alive

The tragedy of life is what dies inside a man while he lives.
ALBERT EINSTEIN

The butterfly counts not months but moments,
and has time enough.
RABINDRANATH TAGORE

Karl Mannfeld came to see me at the recommendation of a member of his church. His wife, Gretta, came with him. They were an easy couple to talk to, and they seemed to have been at each other's side always. They knew each other so well, had grown so close during their thirty years of marriage, that for all practical purposes, they were one. She would feel the arthritis in his knees, and he would suffer her disappointments at missing a dinner date because of his travel.

Karl was the fifty-four-year-old executive of an engineering firm, and a native of Germany. He had married a schoolteacher from his hometown, and some twenty-five years before I met him, they had moved to the States to start a business, a family, and a life together. While they became naturalized citizens of the United States and took great pride in their adoptive country, home was still in Germany, where generations of roots had drawn nourishment. It had always been Karl's intention, and promise, to visit twice each year, but his last trip home had been five years earlier. As his mother grew old, the pull from the homeland strengthened, as did his frustration at never being able to find the time.

He traveled for work once or twice each week, and when in town, typically spent twelve-hour days at the office to compensate for the lost productivity on the road. Gretta would make lunch for both of them and they would eat in his office, not out of thrift, but to capture what time they could together. His work was demanding, but the tedium of each day was broken by brief but regular calls from home. He referred to them as his lifelines in choppy waters.

Gretta and Karl had two children, a boy who looked like him, and a girl every bit her mother. Gretta attended the ball games, supervised the homework, chaperoned the parties, and even learned how to go camping while pretending to enjoy it. Karl's mornings typically started before the kids were up, and only in their teen years were they still awake when he returned from work. In the blink of an eye they grew up. He recalled tears in his eyes when driving his youngest to college one fall day, reflecting on where their youth had gone, on where his youth had gone.

Their friendships were really Gretta's friendships. Karl went along for the ride when he was home, but he found comfort in knowing that other people cared for Gretta almost as much as he did. They attended church together when they could, but it was Gretta who would make it important to their family. As the children grew older and required less of her time, she found the rewards of service through the church and the community.

Karl's passions were history and genealogy. His study was a sanctuary for dusty old texts of years gone by, and a page or two from one of those volumes would bring each of his days to a close. A huge map of the world, yellowing with age, covered one entire wall. Colored pins marked cemeteries, battlefields, and historical sites to explore. Though the pins increased in number, the photo albums recording family trips did not.

Though his job demanded sacrifices insatiably, it had provided them with a good life. Their children had gone to the best of schools, had wanted for no material thing, and the family enjoyed all the extras that Karl's long hours made possible. They had done well financially, planned wisely, and were poised to turn that sacrifice into a bountiful harvest. Karl would retire at fifty-seven, and he and Gretta would spend half of each year traveling. They had designed their retirement home together and had already found the property along a quiet lake on which to build. Through the years of postponing life, that map on the study wall had kept them focused on the promise of tomorrow. Each night they fell off to sleep talking about one of those pins, and the wonders that they would soon explore together.

I was struck by their partnership on that first visit. He attributed his success to her, and she seemed embarrassed by the abundance that they had attracted in a world full of scarcity. Like most people meeting a new physician for the first time, they seemed a little uncomfortable. It quickly became apparent, however, that it was not a diagnosis or talk of a procedure that left them ill at ease. They simply were not used to being the focus of conversation. They much preferred talking about the photographs that decorated my office wall.

Karl was looking for a new primary care physician. I wasn't sure about Gretta, but I had the feeling that she was going to see how things fared with her husband before taking the plunge herself. It was not the first time that I had found myself auditioning for a patient, but I suspected that there was not much about my professional life that they had not already researched thoroughly. They were much more interested in the books that I read, the music I enjoyed, and the world that I saw through a camera lens. They were breathless with delight in learning that the origins of my family name were Swiss. That made us practically neighbors.

I guided our discussion to Karl's health by looking at the list of medications that he was taking. I learned early in my career that a medication list is the summary of one's health. A momentary glance told me that Karl had high blood pressure, elevated cholesterol, gout, and difficulty with seasonal allergies. The various vitamins and herbal preparations on the list suggested that he was proactive about his health, and perhaps open to alternatives not always embraced by traditional medicine. I found the item of the greatest interest at the bottom of the list. In a different color of ink, almost as an afterthought, was written *Depot Lupron*, an injection received every three months.

"So, Mr. Mannfeld," I observed, "you have prostate cancer."

Either the words themselves or the abruptness of their use took them by surprise, for they both jumped a little. "Yes," he slowly replied, casting a glance at his wife, "I was told about six months ago, but I've probably had it a lot longer."

"Were you having problems, or did your doctor just find it?" I asked.

With a deep breath of resignation, Karl told his story. "My company purchased disability insurance for the senior management, and we all had to have physicals. Gretta was thrilled. She had wanted me to have a complete physical for a long time, but our family doctor didn't believe in doing a lot of testing. We didn't even have to pay for it.

"A colonoscopy was part of the physical, and afterwards the doctor asked me when the last time my doctor had examined my prostate. I told him that I had never had a prostate exam, and what did that have to do with a colonoscopy? He said that he had difficulty passing the instrument and felt something unusual when he examined me. He ordered an ultrasound and gave me the name of an urologist for me to see after the test."

It was easy for Karl and Gretta to discount the concerns of a doctor that they didn't know, particularly when an insurance company was paying the bill. Karl felt fine, and it never occurred to him that something could be wrong. Still, he didn't want the company to lose out on the insurance, so he scheduled the ultrasound, but decided he would find his own urologist.

Gretta went with him to see the urologist, and together they would learn the results of the ultrasound. The ultrasound was indeed abnormal and a biopsy was taken that very day, before either of them could even contemplate that their future might look very different. As they drifted off to sleep that night, they found comfort in thoughts of retirement and travel, just thirty months away.

Together they learned about prostate cancer and the need for haste. The pathologist, yet another unknown face with extraordinary power to influence fate, reported that the tumor was a high-grade malignancy, one with great proclivity to aggressively spread. Together they waited for the CT scan, the lessons from earlier that day incessantly replaying in their thoughts, that surgery and cure could be possible if the tumor had not spread. But it had spread. It had spread a great deal. Together they drove home in stunned silence. Like a haunting melody, the survival statistics played over and over again in their minds. They would find no comfort in thoughts of retirement and travel that night.

The following months would be difficult—difficult for Karl to endure, but even more difficult for Gretta to watch him endure. As the spread of the tumor had removed surgery as an option, all their hopes were cast upon chemotherapy. The chemotherapy made Karl ill, and he was forced to face demons from his past. Since he had been a small boy growing up in Germany, one of his greatest fears had been vomiting. He would gladly take fever, the worst of coughs, and a body racked with aches if only he could avoid vomiting. It wasn't rational, but it was a part of his life. The nausea started within minutes after the first dose of chemotherapy was infused into his veins. It was followed shortly by vomiting of an intensity and duration that Karl's darkest dreams could not have conjured. His abdomen was sore for days after each treatment, the vomiting proving a more effective exercise than any evil machine at the gym.

Most fears subside when they are confronted, but Karl's fear flourished and kept watch over his life like a vulture soaring overhead. It followed him around, lashing out when he least expected it. Reminders of the chemotherapy treatment room were everywhere—in the Muzak playing in the elevator at work, in the mauve-colored walls in the conference room, and even in the acetone his wife used painting her nails—each capable of generating intense waves of nausea in the blink of an eye.

The chemotherapy was hard work, perhaps the most important investment toward their futures, and both of them endured it together. Karl's investment was tracked by monthly

CT scans. They had hoped for a better return, but after three months of chemotherapy, there was no change in the tumor. Perhaps this was a good thing, his doctors suggested, since the tumor had not increased in size. Considering how ill the chemotherapy made Karl, however, there seemed to be little benefit in continuing it. The battle would be waged hormonally. Every three months, Karl would receive an injection of medication to stop his body from making testosterone, the stimulus for prostate growth as well as the cancer.

Karl had received his second injection just the week before that initial visit to my office. The injections could elevate blood pressure, and his urologist urged him to see his regular doctor. Karl hadn't seen his family doctor since his diagnosis, and Gretta felt that it was time that they made a change. Karl had difficulty, however, in understanding why he needed to worry about such things as blood pressure and cholesterol. These were concerns for people with futures.

His blood pressure was indeed elevated, and I recommended adjustments to his medications. During those early days, Karl, with Gretta always at his side, would return every couple of weeks so that I could monitor his blood pressure. It provided an opportunity to get to know them better, and more importantly, for them to get to know me. Something troubled me about them, and I feared that I was missing something important. While I had learned a lot about them, I realized that I didn't know much of them. The knowledge of their true selves was something that they shared only with each other, but perhaps that was what I had felt. Their sharing had stopped.

Gretta seldom spoke about herself during their visits, but it was clear that she carried a heavy burden hidden somewhere beneath the smile and apparent self-assuredness. When I inquired about how life was going at home, she promptly replied that things were fine—Karl had his work, and she was busy at church. They looked away when I brought up their travel plans, and each looked very lonely, not like a couple, but like individuals who had forgotten what it was like to be alone. Their lunches at the office together had stopped, and it had been many months since they had drifted off to sleep with talk of home and plans to wander places of wonder.

"You look like you have a lot on your mind, Gretta. Will you share it with me?" I asked softly. She sat in silence, a silence that begged for pity, and I started to regret my intrusion. Tears ran gently down her face. She touched her face softly and looked down at the moistness of her hand, not with embarrassment, but almost with disbelief.

"I haven't been able to cry since this started," she whispered.

Perhaps it was a moment of weakness, or of trust, but the cover of the book had cracked open a bit and I was determined to get a look inside. "Why haven't you been able to cry?" I probed further.

Her eyes flashed in startled recognition, as if she had always known the answer, but never pondered the question. "I'm so angry," she said. "I wake up with anger and go to bed with even more anger. I even feel angry at church. I can't feel anything else. I don't want to feel anything else. Karl's doctor never examined him, never checked his blood. This could have been found earlier, when there was hope for cure. He took away all of our plans. He stole our future."

"You must be pretty angry too," I asked a stunned-looking Karl.

"Perhaps a little," he said. "Mainly, I just feel guilty. Look at what I've done to those I've loved the most. My children grew up without a father, and my wife has waited until tomorrow to live, except there's not going to be a tomorrow. And since I started those shots, I can't even show her the love that I feel, and that she deserves."

Anger and guilt—I can't think of darker emotions or thoughts with lower energy. This was the sadness that I had felt around them. It was the cloud darkening their lives which would no doubt be more deadly to those lives than the tumor that seemed unstoppable. But their admissions gave them something to talk about, something to work on. I struggled to find words of comfort, words that would help them make sense of all that had happened, but I could not. I had seen it too often before, and medicine had not provided me with the wisdom of why bad things happen to good people. The lives that had moved in and out of my life over the years, however, had taught me an important truth. Life is short and there is no promise of tomorrow.

"Gretta, Karl," I started slowly, "I'm so very sorry for what has happened to you. I'm not going to tell you that I understand what you are going through, because I can't. I see a lot of suffering in medicine, but I also see a lot of happiness, happiness that I would never experience today if I focused on the suffering I saw yesterday. I have come to appreciate the wisdom of uncertainty. I could die in an automobile accident tonight, but I am still planning on coming to work tomorrow. More men with prostate cancer die of heart disease than of their cancer. We just don't know what tomorrow will bring. That can either frighten us away from making the most of today, or excite us into experiencing every moment that today offers.

"Six months ago you had fabulous plans to travel, and to share every moment together. What has really changed? The future was as uncertain then as it is now, but still you dreamed. Live that dream today."

When they left the office that day, I didn't think that I would see them again. That would have been a loss since I liked them a lot. They had both seemed quite upset, however, and not quite ready to come to terms with the issues I had forced to the surface. The following week Gretta called to cancel their follow-up appointments, and while she didn't explain, the reason seemed obvious. The thought that I had hurt them troubled me greatly. They were difficult people to forget and I would frequently find them in my thoughts.

Over a month had passed when an envelope arrived with the office mail bearing a strange postmark and unfamiliar, colorful stamps. Inside was a photograph of an office building, perhaps ten stories high. In large letters across the top of the structure was inscribed my family's name. Enclosed was also a handwritten note:

> *Karl has retired and we have been home for several weeks now. Shortly after arriving we saw this building near the airport. Karl was so excited that he stopped the car to take this picture. We saw it as a message.*
>
> *In an old cemetery outside of Königsee, generations of ancestors spoke to us while the beauty of the Alps filled us with peace and touched us with Spirit.*
>
> *We are living our dream.*
> *Gretta*

Every few weeks a postcard would arrive from a different spot on the globe. Dunkirk, St. Petersburg, Tokyo, Manila, Peking, Honolulu, Gettysburg. Each would be unsigned and inscribed with three simple words: *Living the Dream*.

Seven months after I had last seen them, the Mannfelds were again sitting in my office. They beamed in delight when I pointed to the corkboard on the wall that displayed the photograph and postcards that they had sent. I asked if they had run out of places to go, and with amused faces both stroked their chins as if pondering the mystery of life. It was autumn, and they were looking forward to spending the end of the year with their family. Great adventures would await in the new year.

We spoke of genealogy and the historical richness of Europe. They urged me to seek my own family's origins, surprised at the number of times that they had encountered my family name while roaming Germany and Switzerland. We spoke of historical landmarks and the indescribable power one feels standing amid the timeless. We spoke of blood pressure, cholesterol, and medication refills. We spoke of their afternoon plans to take an excited grandson to the zoo. But it was Karl who was most excited, as it would be his first trip. We spoke of many things that day, but we did not speak of cancer.

Winter came early that year, and by mid-November a thick cover of snow had softened our world, more snow than most winters brought during the entire season. With the snow came grumbling patients, stressed from difficult commutes, children home from school, and winter colds. The snow also brought Karl to the office, with a smile as broad as the snow was deep. He had hurt his back, either from shoveling his driveway or cross-country skiing with Gretta. It was more than a fair trade, Karl observed. It had been years since he had had the time to clear his own drive, and he hadn't been on skis since his childhood in the Alps. He had had a ball.

Several days later, Gretta called to tell us that medication, hot soaks, and stretching was not helping Karl's back. In fact, his pain was worse. His medication was changed, but I grew concerned when he failed to show improvement after several more days. The back X-ray that I had ordered was normal, but I had a horrible feeling that there was more to the story, and that it would not read well. I was grateful that Karl and Gretta did not seem to understand the significance of the bone scan that I ordered, and I was careful not to volunteer any suspicion or fear.

The night before Thanksgiving found me standing in a deserted radiology department with Karl's bone scan spread out before me. The radiologists had long since gone home, but I would not need their help interpreting this study. Prostate cancer favors bone as a place to spread, and it had found great prosperity in the person of Karl Mannfeld. Spine, hips, pelvis, shoulders, skull—the tumor was everywhere. I was amazed that Karl only had back pain.

Thanksgiving was not a time for bad news. It had been a much-anticipated day for the Mannfelds. Three generations would spend the day together. The past had brought them abundance, but its acquisition had never seemed as satisfying as the chase. Business, at least successful business, knew no holidays, and at the time providing for the family had seemed a greater priority than spending time as a family. This year they would experience a different kind of abundance—time to spend together.

The day after Thanksgiving I made a rare house call. The office was closed, but I needed to see Karl and Gretta. It would not be a conversation that we would have over the telephone, although the opportunity the phone offered to lighten the burden that I felt would have been welcomed. There was an uncomfortable familiarity in standing on their doorstep, and my thoughts drifted back to an earlier Thanksgiving, my first as a doctor. My recollection of that VA hospital was eerily vivid, and the similarities seemed much more than coincidence could arrange. While the years had given me practice dispensing bad news, it never got easier. I had always thought that it would.

Karl and Gretta were delighted to see me, but didn't seem all that surprised. I was relieved that Karl's pain was under better control and that it had not dampened a wonderful holiday with his family. They had even joined him on a long walk in the woods, and while the going was slow, each step was something more for them to share.

It was over a cup of coffee that I told Karl that the cancer had spread to his bones and that this was why he had pain. Radiation to his back would be very effective in treating the pain, but it would not change the outcome. Gretta and Karl seemed to be expecting the news, and received it with a calmness that almost seemed rehearsed. Karl asked the question that I had been dreading, but that I knew would come. "How long do I have?"

"I don't know, Karl," I said looking him in the eye. "I can give you statistics and make a guess, but frankly, I'm always wrong. I haven't the knowledge or the wisdom to answer your question. I think, though, that we are talking weeks to months, not months to years or days to weeks."

With the hint of a grin, Karl glanced at Gretta and said, "The urologist would have given me a date, and then he would have been mad as hell if I made him wrong."

"It's better this way, not knowing," he seemed to think out loud. "Otherwise, I'd always be thinking about tomorrow."

Karl wanted to think about the radiation. If it meant less pain medication, it sounded pretty good. He hated the thought of drowsiness stealing from his days, as the pain medication had done over the previous week. He and Gretta would think it all over later, but at that moment, he much preferred to talk about their trip. And so we did. Through several hours, hundreds of photographs, dozens of maps, and a lunch, Karl and Gretta reveled in the sharing of the places that set their spirits free.

When the door closed behind me, I stood on that porch for the second time that day and paused in reflection. There was an almost mystical contrast between the dread and pain that I had felt earlier and the peace that now filled me completely. It was then that I realized that the anger and guilt that I had seen before, and had feared today, was missing in Gretta and Karl. All I had sensed was peace, and they had shared it with me.

Karl got the radiation treatments to his back, and it worked quite well. On most days he didn't need any pain medication. I was surprised but grateful that the other bones that the cancer had spread to weren't causing pain. Unfortunately, the radiation oncologist who treated Karl couldn't resist the temptation to diagnose, even when diagnosis was no longer helpful. A CT scan revealed that the tumor had also invaded Karl's liver and occupied a large proportion of his lungs. It was a detail that Karl was unconcerned about. He felt well enough to go about his daily routine, and that was all that was important. He always had been a big-picture kind of guy.

I would not see Karl again until Christmas Eve, when on a whim, I stopped by to see how he was doing. There was little that I could do in the office that couldn't be accomplished on home visits or by telephone, so I wanted to spare Karl office visits and the illusion of being a patient. The family had already gathered for the holiday. His eyes sparkled with the anticipation of Christmas, the same sparkle that I could see in his grandson's eyes. Karl denied feeling pain or having a care in the world. He looked more tired than I had seen him before, but Gretta told me that he had been hard at work all day decorating for Christmas. As I turned to leave, Karl rummaged about under the Christmas tree and surfaced with a small package that he pressed into my hands. With an arm around my shoulder, he pulled me close and whispered into my ear, "Thank you."

Standing on their porch, I was again visited by the past. In the warm glow cast from the holiday lights I examined the porcelain figurine that I held close. Made by hand in Germany, carried with love across the continents, that Carolina wren reached deep into my earliest memories of medicine, and touched my heart. Coincidence? I thought it was more.

I would not speak with Karl again. Five days later I received a call from the emergency department. While walking with Gretta, Karl had become acutely short of breath and collapsed. The emergency medicine doc thought that he had suffered a large blood clot to his lungs, not an uncommon event with cancer patients. Without placing him on a ventilator, it would be unlikely that Karl would survive, but such care could only prolong his life, not heal him. We would keep Karl comfortable, but we would not intrude upon his journey.

By the time I made it to the hospital, most of Karl's family had arrived and gathered around his bed, with Gretta at its head. Karl appeared quite comfortable, almost like he was in a deep sleep. His breathing was shallow, but not labored. It was a peace that I had hoped for for Karl, but hadn't known how to provide. I took notice of all the tear-filled eyes that watched over Karl that day. One pair belonged to me.

Gretta wrapped her arm around my waist, hugged me close, and held me there. "Don't be sad," she said. "Karl lived his dream. He retired before his fifty-fifth birthday. He walked the battlefields of Normandy, Gettysburg, Verdun, and Waterloo. He learned how to fish at a pond with a grandson at his side. He learned how to squeeze the last drop of life from every day. And he shared every moment with me.

"You say that you are not wise, but yet you helped us see uncertainty as a precious gift. We could have spent the rest of our time together dreaming. You helped us turn from the past so that we could have the present, and there we found our dreams. I was once so angry that our future had been stolen from us, but the thief was the anger that blinded us to the only thing that we had really ever had, the present moment.

"Standing in that cemetery it all became so clear. The answers we sought could not be found in the generations before us, or in the promise of things to come. The answer was the Spirit we felt there, the peace that hung over those Alps like early morning fog. The answer was in reaching out and grasping what had always walked with us, now and then. As we learned to do that, each moment was timeless. There was always now. We had forever to have each other."

Gretta placed her hands on each side of my face. They were trembling slightly. Her eyes were filled with tears, yet I did not sense grief. Reaching up on her toes, she softly kissed my forehead. "Karl's retirement lasted an eternity," she said. "Thank you for blessing our lives."

Karl passed quietly, and in peace, a short time later. His family was at his side. The Carolina wren still sits on my desk, and often reminds me of the lessons that Karl taught me about time, embracing life, and the power of adversity. Without cancer, Karl might never have lived. He might never have retired while he was still alive.

CHAPTER 6

We Do Not Have Much Time

We usually lose today, because there has been a yesterday,
and tomorrow is coming.
JOHANN WOLFGANG VON GOETHE

Time is but the stream I go fishing in. I drink at it, but while
I drink I see the sandy bottom and detect how shallow it is.
Its thin current slides away, but eternity remains.
HENRY DAVID THOREAU

Everywhere I go, I see my patients. Many of my colleagues would call that the curse of living where you practice, but one man's curse is another's blessing. Perhaps there are costs, but living among people that you care for has shown me a face of medicine that few get to know. Much of medicine is routine, but the ordinary has a way of becoming extraordinary when your patients are your neighbors. The routine blood pressure check becomes the plumber down the street; the heart failure patient is that man you see walking his dog every morning; that lady with gout delivers your mail. The routine becomes personal, and somewhere during the transition it becomes special.

The barbershop, the hardware store, and even the coffee shop become places from which some of my best understanding of people flows. The grocery store has been a particularly deep well from which to draw awareness. I'm always amused by the patients who try to hide the contents of their shopping carts, or those curious to know what their doctor takes home to eat. It is in those brief moments that we stand and chat, however, that we are closest and we share the most.

There is a spot in that grocery store that protects a special memory for me, like the lingering taste from a rich pastry. To the right of the cheese, left of the butter, and not far from the baked goods, I can almost see the stain on the floor left by the egg that crashed there many years ago. Invariably, the memory is accompanied by the image of Helen Derickson. It is a powerful remembrance. I can see her standing there. I can even smell her perfume.

It seems like just the other day that I stood in that spot, inspecting a carton of eggs before placing them in my basket. It had been a long day and I was late getting home, but not too late to forgo the rituals of shopping that my mother had instilled in me. Lost in my task, I didn't see the older lady in the fur coat walk up to me, at least, not until two furry arms reached around me and squeezed me tight.

"How are you, how are you!" screeched a delighted voice.

Startled, I allowed three of the eggs in my custody to make a break for it. One I managed to catch, one made a soft landing on my shoe and rolled safely to freedom, but the third came to a spectacular finish across the tiled floor.

"Oh well," Helen said, looking down at the remnants of what I had planned to have for tomorrow's breakfast. "It was too high in cholesterol anyway."

She chuckled at her own joke and, without a moment's pause, continued. "I was just thinking about you, and there you stood! I worry about you so much. Are you eating enough? You look so thin. Are you getting enough rest? You look so tired."

This lady could have been my mother, but her bubbly personality made me smile. It was good to see Helen happy, even if I was embarrassed by the attention. I had not always known her as a happy person, and she had not always taken such notice of others. It was a metamorphosis that I had learned from, and it had changed me.

Medicine had brought many teachers to me, each sharing a truth that guided me on my journey. Helen became a special teacher. She would teach through change, and the lessons would resonate beyond life itself. Encounters with former teachers started to seem a little less random, a little less serendipitous after I met Helen. She beckoned me toward a trust in the existence of a higher intelligence, one that knows how to contact us.

My early days with Helen were difficult. We mixed like oil and water. I found myself dreading her visits, which seemed far too frequent, I thought, no doubt calculated just to antagonize me. I would be the latest in a long line of physicians from whom she had sought care, and the warning bells rang loud in my mind.

That first visit will be seared into my memory forever, a backdrop that makes the lessons that followed seem miraculous. I had asked Helen, "How is it that you came to see me?"

"Put the conceit on hold, doc," she replied with a look of disgust. "It certainly wasn't because anyone thought you were good. I picked your name out of the phone book as the shortest drive from home. You can't be any worse than the others, and if you are, there are a lot more names in that book."

My shock must have appeared obvious as she looked at her watch and continued, "Can we just get on with it? I don't want to spend all day here. Some of us have to work for a living."

This was a new experience for me. Not that I expected everyone to like me, but most did. I had never experienced such hostility directed towards me, and that it came from a stranger made it feel all the more cold and caustic. But there was another insight that was new for me. The good opinion of others seemed important to me.

Within sixty seconds, this lady had me angry and defensive. I'm not sure what bothered me more, her comments and attitude, or my reaction to them. I had dealt with difficult patients before, but I had always found a foundation for communication, and if not agreement, at least understanding. In that instant, I considered closing the chart and suggesting that she look elsewhere for a physician. I suspected that that had been her fate with previous doctors, and it would have been the easy path to take then. Perhaps I would have done so had it not been for those earlier teachers. Perhaps some of their lessons lingered, dormant, waiting for such an opportunity.

"Mrs. Derickson," I calmly replied, "you have a choice whether or not to come here. I have a choice as well, and right now, I'm choosing to forgive those comments. I know nothing about you from which to judge, or even understand. You know nothing about me. But we need to find that understanding; otherwise, I cannot help you. I'm willing to try."

She came right back at me, almost with a practiced ease. "Doc, I don't need your understanding, nor is it welcome. What I need is your scribble so that I can buy my medicine. It's bad enough that people are cheated by the pharmacies and drug companies, but to have to pay you for the honor is despicable."

This was going to be one tough lady. But she was also a lady in need. Her blood pressure was horrible, her lungs were ravaged by emphysema, and heart failure had filled her tissues with fluid. I feared that her needs would exceed my capacity to give, but I felt drawn to try.

On that very first visit I was struck by how important the past was in Helen's life. She never spoke of future plans, and discussions about the present always revolved around years past. The present was always unpleasant and difficult for Helen, and she was able to trace the roots of each of her problems to wounds that the past had inflicted. I asked her once if she was depressed.

"You would be depressed too, if you had had my life," she stated emphatically. "I was pregnant and had three children when my husband left me. I knew my life was over then and there, and I was absolutely right."

Every problem had a cause and someone to blame for it. The stress of her job gave her high blood pressure. She grew up in a home of smokers, so naturally she became one. When she wanted to quit, the tobacco companies made sure that she was addicted. Her parents did not place a high value on education, so the only job she could get without college was as a secretary. The list went on and on, and she readily shared it with others, often. It became quickly apparent that Helen was a prisoner of her past.

Some say that no good deed ever goes unpunished, and in Helen's case I wondered if it might not be true. I would regret my decision to keep her as a patient at least once every visit during those early days. Every visit was a battle. Her blood pressure was as stubborn as she, and every medication change, every suggestion was resisted and fought. Every medication was too expensive for her, and offered proof of doctors' insensitivity to those of limited means. Every test was questioned as excessive, necessary only for my financial gain. Every ache, every pain, every bad day was a side effect of her medication and proof of malpractice.

It is said that we can give others only what we have ourselves. The discomfort I felt during Helen's visits seemed trivial compared to the pain that I could see in her eyes, and that which must have filled her soul. I began to feel sorry for Helen, and I was rather embarrassed that it had taken me so long to start seeing the person behind that reluctant patient. The bitterness and sadness that I could see in the office, no doubt, lived with her daily, and it was the face that others saw.

With each visit, a small piece of the puzzle that was Helen Derickson would fit into place. Helen had lived alone since her youngest child left home after high school graduation, over forty years earlier. Her children all lived nearby, but visits frequently caused clashes between strong personalities and they had become rare in recent years. She had several grandchildren, but their lives were a mystery. She passed her time by going to work—not that she liked her work, but it represented a lesser evil than being home. She tolerated weekends and holidays, but the thought of retirement terrified her. She actually took some degree of comfort in her health problems. Perhaps she would not live to see retirement.

Though I thought it would be the death of me, or that of my office staff, Helen's blood pressure gradually came under control. There were plenty of problems to take its place. I was particularly concerned with her emphysema and the clinical decline that I could see with almost every office visit. I suspected that she had pulmonary hypertension and wanted her to see her pulmonologist. It was yet another battle to get Helen to agree to go. Her shortness of breath was as stubborn as she was, however, and it would become more persuasive than my arguments. After several months of holding out, Helen finally relented and promised to make an appointment.

To my dismay, Helen called a few days later to report that the specialist refused to give her an appointment. She had an outstanding balance from years previous and would not be scheduled an appointment until it was paid. Helen was adamant that she owed them nothing and she reveled in the role of victim. She would not pay the greedy doctor a cent, even if it would cost her her life.

I had struggled far too long with Helen to be outdone by a scheduling clerk. But nothing was easy with Helen, and my office staff's attempts to intervene with the specialist failed to win an appointment. Even my personal calls would go no further than the office manager. I was astonished to learn that the obstacle to care was thirty-two dollars not paid by insurance years earlier. But I also suspected that Helen's past was again haunting her, and no doubt her previous behavior at the specialist's office left them uninspired to help her now. To the dismay of my staff, I wrote the specialist a personal check and sent it to his home by overnight mail. The next day we heard from Helen. She gloated that she had won her battle. She had an appointment with the specialist.

Helen and I would never speak about that check. It was to be a secret, but I learned that she was told of it when she kept her appointment with the specialist. Helen seemed different on the very next office visit. The hostility was gone. Her voice seemed less sharp. It was an amazing transformation, one that

I expected would be fleeting, but it endured and strengthened. We started to learn about each other, more than what was required for a patient-physician relationship, more of what friends would know of each other.

One day Helen lingered for an unusually long period of time in the office after her appointment, almost as if she didn't want to leave, almost as if she was searching for something. She inspected the pictures of birds on my walls and the figurines on my desk. She commented that she had once been a birder and was thinking about taking it up again. I stood in shocked disbelief. We had a common interest. It was the link that I had long looked for, but could never seem to find. When I stopped looking, it found me.

Helen was true to her intention. She found her old bird books, packed away decades earlier, and bought herself a new pair of binoculars. Weekends became something special again, a time when she could venture out and become reacquainted with beauty and wonder. She would sit for hours watching birds, and she found comfort in the quiet.

Helen became a favorite presence in the office. She grew attached to the staff and took an interest in their lives. Each visit, she would bring them something from the bakery, and she took delight in their pleasure. She started to arrive early for her appointments and was always content sitting in the waiting room, frequently engaging others in conversation. The Helen Derickson we had once known was no more.

As months turned into years, the bitter old lady was forgotten. The caterpillar had turned into a beautiful butterfly. Her lung disease would eventually require oxygen, and she accepted the news without anger and blame. "Nobody put those cigarettes in my mouth," she would tell me. Instead, she was grateful that portable oxygen could keep her with her birds and out among nature. She must have been quite a sight—sitting on a log, tethered to an oxygen tank, peering into the trees with binoculars. But what a wonderful sight it would be.

The winter months were difficult for Helen. During the cold and flu season I would see her every couple of weeks in the hopes of heading off pneumonia or any exacerbation of her emphysema. On one such visit, Helen seemed unusually short of breath after walking the short distance from the waiting room. She had felt bad for a number of days, but did not call for fear that she would be hospitalized. Helen hated the hospital and would do anything to avoid going there. When I told her that I suspected pneumonia, she pleaded not to be admitted and promised faithful compliance with any instruction if she could go home. It was a side of Helen that I had not seen before. It wasn't the stubbornness that I had once known, but more fear, almost terror. I was reminded of a small child, horribly afraid of the dark, just before the bedroom light was turned off.

I put my arm around Helen to offer some comfort and noticed that she was trembling. "Okay, Helen. We'll try it your way. I'll give you some antibiotics and increase your breathing medicine, but if you are not getting any better by tomorrow, we need to think about the hospital. It's not like you haven't been there before. You will do fine."

"Not this time," she whispered with tears in her eyes. It was the first time that I had ever seen her cry.

The ringing of the telephone woke me abruptly at five o'clock the following morning. It was Helen, and she could hardly breathe, unable to speak in full sentences. She had sat up all night hoping that her medicine would bring her a miracle, but it did not come. I told her to call 911 and that I would see her at the hospital. The absence of argument reflected the severity of her illness, and I was worried.

Helen was already in the emergency room by the time I made it to the hospital. She arrived in respiratory failure and was promptly placed on a ventilator. Her chest X-ray showed pneumonia, as I had feared, but I had seen far worse. With the severity of her pulmonary disease, however, Helen was always just one infection away from respiratory failure. She was admitted to the intensive care unit, where I would see her three times a day.

The first few days, there wasn't much to do except wait. The intravenous lines would provide her antibiotics and some nutrition, the ventilator would support her respiratory system, and the nurses would provide the other essentials of life. Time, powers beyond my control, and understanding would do the healing. The longer I practiced medicine, the more this healing thing fascinated me, and the more I realized that I was an observer to it, rather than a cause of it.

The ventilator had silenced Helen and took away the tool I used the most, listening. In the ICU I was reduced to physical examination and reviewing data from machines and laboratory studies. It would never tell me as much as listening to a patient's story and feeling the power behind that story. Perhaps that is why I had always felt comfortable in the ICU during those early days as a resident. I hadn't learned to listen and much preferred a silenced patient to one who distracted me from all of that data. Standing by Helen's bed, the ICU now seemed a foreign place, almost an obstacle to healing.

Technology seemed determined to take away what little closeness was possible in the ICU and keep doctors apart from our patients. The monitors that had once revealed only cardiac rhythm were replaced with machines to report vital signs, produce electrocardiograms, and even measure oxygen in the blood stream, all at a glance. The ventilator had become more a computer than the simple breathing machine of my training, calculating respiratory parameters at the push of a button. IV poles had been replaced with electronics that could control every drop of fluid and medication that entered the patient's veins. Even the beds were smart, continuously reporting the body weight and caloric requirements of their sickened occupants. With all this technology, nurses could be more efficient and care for more patients. But technology couldn't provide a human touch or a knowing presence, and I wondered, at what cost had our medical advancements come?

Over the following days, the clearing chest X-ray and falling white blood cell count told me that Helen's pneumonia was getting better, but she remained stubbornly dependent on the ventilator. Aerosolized medications delivered directly to the lungs, massive doses of steroids, and frequent suctioning of the airways had produced only a modicum of improvement. She was far from being able to breathe on her own and being weaned from the machine. By the fifth day on the ventilator I began to worry whether or not she would ever come off. The tube that had been inserted into her airway when she was placed on the ventilator would soon start to damage her larynx, and the pulmonary consultants recommended a tracheostomy. They would create a hole in her neck that would enable the ventilator to be connected directly to the trachea so it could be left in place indefinitely, if need be. Helen could then be moved to an extended care facility, where, hopefully, she could be weaned from the ventilator in time.

As difficult as it was to see Helen on the ventilator at all, the idea of her permanently tethered to a machine in a nursing home was an image incompatible with the lady I had come to know so well. I would give her a couple more days. All of my medical tricks had been expended and the consultants saw little to encourage us. I could offer her nothing more than the chance to get better. The healing would have to come from a different place, a place that I suspected was within Helen, a place that the consultants knew little of.

By the following morning, the LED display on the ventilator flashed encouragement, albeit subtle encouragement. The parameters we used to gauge whether she was ready to be weaned, while far from endorsing life off the machine, were decisively better. The consultants saw trivial change and wishful thinking, standing firm on their prognostications. But there was more. Helen remained sedated and could not speak, and her physical examination had changed little over the past week, but standing by her side I knew something was different. It was as if that communication that I had longed for and could not find had found me, but at a level beyond words, beyond thought, and beyond my understanding. I knew Helen was getting better.

With every hour of that day the numbers looked better. The improvement was incremental, but no longer trivial. By the next day, Helen was off the ventilator. By that night, she was sitting up in a chair. By the following day she was walking with assistance and talking up a storm. When the talk turned to birds I knew that Helen was back. While the consultants could not explain her rapid and unexpected recovery, they nonetheless took credit for it, their egos bathing in success.

I arrived at the hospital early the following morning. Helen no longer needed intensive care, and I wanted to get the paperwork done to transfer her to a regular hospital bed before I had to leave for the office. Outside Helen's room an excited group of nurses had gathered, their hushed tones growing silent as I approached.

"What's wrong?" I asked, sounding concerned and a little paranoid at the same time.

"Oh, she's fine, doctor," the charge nurse said in a calming voice. "It's just been a strange night around here."

"Define strange?" I asked, feeling a little left out of the fun.

"We looked in on Mrs. Derickson at about five this morning and she wasn't in her bed. We couldn't find her on the unit. The unit clerk saw a bright flash of light in her room and when we went to investigate, there she was, sitting up in bed looking as peaceful as could be."

"What was the light?" I asked, disappointed that the strange wasn't sounding all that strange.

"We were afraid it was a fire because there was a hint of smoke in the air. When we asked Helen about it, she said that Father Mike had visited and brought incense. She described him right down to the birthmark on his forehead."

"Maybe he was in early for someone else who was sick and just stopped by," I suggested.

"Doctor," the charge nurse paused for a deep, patient breath, "Father Mike died five years ago."

The story had just turned strange. The nurses were thrilled by my look of disbelief, finding great satisfaction in my inability to offer a logical explanation for the happenings a couple of hours earlier. But a logical explanation had to exist. Older people hallucinate all the time when they are sick in the hospital. Perhaps she had met this priest before, or had seen a photograph of him. The smoke thing, well, that would have to wait until I had more time to think.

As I turned to enter Helen's room, the nurse taking care of her surprised me with a question. "Is your father well, doctor?"

"Yes, at least I think so. Why do you ask?"

"Oh, no reason in particular," she commented as we walked in to see Helen together.

Helen looked absolutely great. You never would have known she had been so ill. I was intrigued by what one of the nurses had said, about her looking peaceful. That was exactly how Helen looked, so much so that I felt at peace just being in her room, quite a change from the time-pressured haste I had felt just moments earlier. Her room was much different from what I had known during most of her stay. The monitor was dark, the IV controllers gone, and the ventilator pushed into a corner, their technology useless among the healthy.

What intrigued me the most was the display of cards that covered most of one wall. I hadn't noticed them before. There were dozens of them. One large card was signed by more than a hundred different hands, everyone who worked in Helen's office building. Many cards were from children, some signed in crayon. All wished her health and spoke of generosity and gratitude.

Helen looked so good that it seemed like she should be going home rather than moving to another hospital room. We spoke of medications, joked about hospital food, and of course, talked about birds. When she sensed that I was getting ready to leave, her face grew serious.

"There is something I need to tell you," she said, asking and stating it at the same time.

"Why don't I stop by over lunch, Helen," I suggested. "You'll be in your new room and we can sit for a while and talk."

She smiled, but shook her head no. "We do not have much time."

Without waiting for a response from me, she went on. "I've been sitting here thinking about the first time I met you, and all the years that have followed. Of all the souls I have encountered in my life, yours has been my favorite. Despite that, I don't think I have ever thanked you for everything you have done for me. My past was my captor. I've learned that miracles are something that happen now. If you aren't there, you will never experience them, and worse, you will never believe in them. You have made that possible. Thank you."

"I'm just a simple doc, Helen," I commented, my face feeling flushed with embarrassment. "I have no such special powers."

"Yes, you do," she insisted. "We all do, but most of us never realize it or figure out how to use them. I was so afraid of coming to the hospital this time, but what I was frightened of is going to take me to wondrous places. The only thing I worry about now is that someone will try to stop me from moving on. I hope you will help me with that too.

"But there is something else," Helen went on. "I met your dad last night at the gathering. You look so much alike, I knew him right off. He's so very proud of you. I don't think he has gotten used to the idea of moving on yet. He is worried about your mother and doesn't want to leave her alone. I just want you to know that I'll help watch over him until she is ready to join us."

I glanced over at the nurse, who gave me one of those "I told you so" looks. Helen was indeed confused, but I had no desire to challenge her. I thanked her for her comments, gave her a hug, and told her that I would return later. As my hand brushed across her robe, I noticed the bottom of it was damp.

"What happened here?" I asked.

"Oh, I guess the grass was wet last night," she replied calmly.

A cold chill ran through my body and I trembled a bit when I left the room. Perhaps it was my imagination, but I thought I had detected a slight odor of smoke. The nurses were right, it was indeed strange. There were probably better words to explain that morning, but I wasn't ready to accept such possibilities—at least, not then.

Late that morning, I was pulled from an examination room for an urgent call from the hospital. Helen had arrested.

When the transporter arrived to take her to her new room, she was found unconscious, breathless, and without a pulse. The resuscitation team worked on her for more than a half hour before restoring a heart rate. She was back on the ventilator, unresponsive. They were having trouble keeping her blood pressure stable.

By the time I made it back to the hospital, Helen's family had gathered at her bedside. The room lacked the peace I had felt earlier in the day. The machines were back, but they had nothing good to say. Her heart rate was erratic and what blood pressure she had was being maintained by massive quantities of intravenous drugs. The ventilator worked unimpeded, without any resistance from Helen's body. Her pupils were dilated and she lacked any of the reflexes that would tell of brain activity. It was hard to know how long her brain had been deprived of oxygen, but most certainly it had been too long.

I explained all of the machines to the family, and the meaning of what they had to say. I told them of my visit with Helen earlier that day, and her desire that her journey not be delayed. I shared with them my belief that the Helen they knew had already moved on. The family spoke with a single voice, that Helen would want the life support withdrawn.

One of her daughters walked up to me and placed a hand on my shoulder. "Doctor," she said, "thank you for everything you did for Mom. Thank you for being here with us now. Thank you for that tear in your eye."

"I didn't do anything, ma'am," I insisted. "She has been an easy lady to like."

"Didn't do anything? Easy to like? Mom told us about the check. There has been nothing easy about it. She was a mean and bitter woman, at least until she met you. Look at that wall. These are all people that Mom learned to touch.

She certainly didn't get it out of a book. And look at us, all in the same room. We are a family again. You gave our mother back to us, and in the process, you taught us all that life is short. That we can change who we are in a minute."

I waited while everyone said their goodbyes to Helen and then asked the nurse to slowly turn off intravenous medications that were supporting her blood pressure. It was always hard to predict if a patient would breathe on their own for a while after a ventilator was turned off, and I was hoping to spare Helen's family that discomfort. Her blood pressure gradually fell and her heart rate became progressively slow. All eyes became fixed to the monitor. Heads would bob with every beat of the heart. As the heads bobbed slower and slower, I had the nurse turn off the monitor. A few minutes and a nod later, she turned off the ventilator. Helen fell back into that peace I had seen earlier and continued her journey.

I didn't get much work done the rest of that day, spending much of it in the quiet sanctuary of home, lost in thought. And there was much to think about. I thought about that check that I had written almost a decade earlier and forgotten about. Strange that her family would know of it, and speak of it. Could such a small thing touch a life and make a difference? It had been too long ago. Perhaps the check was written not out of kindness but expediency, a thought that bothered me. Helen was one of my many teachers. Never again will I underestimate the power within a simple act of kindness.

I thought about the fear that I saw in Helen that last day in the office, almost as if she had suspected what awaited her at the hospital. But the morning of her death, when she had such a clear vision of what lay ahead, the fear was gone. It was as if she had climbed a high hill and looked down upon the path that she had been taking, clearly seeing where she had come from, and seeing with equal clarity what wonders waited around the next bend and distant rise. And on that hill, perhaps, was the gathering that she had spoken of, where time merged with place and fear was not possible. Perhaps from that dimension she brought back a morsel of the infinite wisdom that can be found there, to share with us so that our journeys might also be on lighted paths. We do not have much time.

We do not have much time. It played over and over again in my mind as I listened to the ring through the telephone receiver. "Dad, just called to see how you were doing."

"What a wonderful surprise. I've been thinking about you all day. I had the strangest dream last night."

CHAPTER 7

God Has Been Good to Me

Gratitude is the fairest blossom which springs from the soul.
HENRY WARD BEECHER

*Gratitude bestows reverence, allowing us to encounter
everyday epiphanies, those transcendent moments of awe
that change forever how we experience life and the world.*
JOHN MILTON

P aul Prescot taught a seminar course on life. There was
no assigned reading, no class schedule, not even papers
to write. It was a field course, filled with the observation of
truths that are seldom recognized as true and experimenting
with new ways to touch that place in others where all of us
are the same. It was a small class, meeting some days in my
office, and other days in a hospital room or in the parking lot
of the local deli. He was one of my best teachers. The teacher-
student ratio was so small that by the time the class neared its
conclusion, we almost seemed as one.

I met Paul Prescot when he came to see me to follow up a recent hospitalization at the teaching hospital. It was the fifth time that he had been given an appointment, but only the first time that he had remained out of the hospital long enough to keep it. While I waited for him to complete paperwork and for my staff to run him through the check-in obstacle course, I sat in my office to start to get to know this most elusive of patients. Multiple hospital admissions generate many reports, each offering insight that might be helpful to establishing a relationship with my new patient.

Eighteen months earlier, this fifty-seven-year-old man had never seen the working side of a hospital gown. In fact, I would be only his second personal physician, and he intended to see me even less than my predecessor, who had retired long before Mr. Prescot's baptismal immersion into modern medicine. His adventure would start at the most unlikely of places, somewhere between the poultry barn and the dairy cattle at the county fair. He had been raised on a farm, and going to the county fair was like going home again. A local hospital had stationed their community outreach van in the middle of the festivities and offered free health screenings. Mr. Prescot tagged along with his wife and waited patiently while she had her blood pressure, cholesterol, and blood sugar measured. A dermatologist scrutinized her face and arms for evidence of skin cancer and declared her concern-free.

"Your husband there, however," she said to Mrs. Prescot, "has a spot on his forehead that I do not like."

She referred Mr. Prescot to a local dermatologist, and several weeks later the spot was excised and biopsied. It was a squamous cell skin cancer. If you had to have cancer, this one wasn't a bad one to have. While the cancer cells could invade adjacent tissues, it almost never spread to other parts of the body and it was almost always cured surgically.

It was hard to think of skin cancer as real cancer, and the Prescots moved on with their lives with little pause, except to start wearing sunblock more and stop working in the garden without hats on. It seemed a shallow gesture, as the decades of work and play in the hot sun had been permanently written into the pages of time. The rituals would remind them from time to time, though, that they needed to find a new doctor.

The county fair was again approaching when Paul started to take notice of headaches that had been sharing his days for many weeks. He usually ignored such things, taking the view that aches and pains were simply distractions from life's work. The headaches gradually worsened over time and spread from the back of his head to his neck and shoulders. When he developed weakness in his right arm, he found it difficult to shake hands, and shaking hands was an important part of his life's work.

Still without a doctor, Paul turned to an urgent care practice not far from his home. The physician thought that the pain and weakness were related to pinched nerves in the neck. Muscle relaxants, anti-inflammatory drugs, and heat were prescribed, and Paul was greatly relieved when he was better within a couple of days. When he awoke one Sunday morning a week or so later, however, unable to move his right arm, he knew that he had more than a pinched nerve. As his wife drove him to the emergency room, fearful of a stroke, he realized that this would be the first time that he had ever missed work.

If there was a time to pick to be a patient in the emergency department of the teaching hospital, it was Sunday morning. It was the one time of the week that the emergency medicine treadmill would slow, allowing time for detailed examinations, thoughtful consideration, and in-depth discussions with concerned families. For medical students and junior residents, it was a great time to learn. Paul was deemed an interesting case. You never wanted to find yourself an interesting case in a teaching hospital.

The medical history and physical exam done by a medical student were repeated by interns, residents, and finally attending physicians. Enough blood was drawn to rival ancient bloodletting rituals. Countless tests were ordered, tests with names so long that they were referred to by initials. It was a strange and alien land that Paul found himself in, and he had difficulty finding the peace that the years had taught him could be found in every situation. Without that peace, fear paid him a visit. It had been a long time since he had known fear, and it came as a fluttering in his chest, a heavy breath, and a fullness in his stomach. His thoughts drifted back to similar feelings as a boy, sitting in a waiting room before having a tooth pulled, feeling very alone. But he was no longer a boy, and he was embarrassed at being frightened. He didn't keep many secrets from his wife, but as they wheeled him away from her on the way to the CT scanner, he worked hard to keep that one.

As Paul rested on the hard surface of the CT scanner, the loud hum from the huge machine his only companion, his doctors practiced tradition. Developing the differential diagnosis, the list of potential causes for Paul's illness, was a skill passed down through generations of physicians. It was the hallmark of medical education, and they took it quite seriously at the teaching hospital. But technology would render tradition moot. The diagnosis fairly leaped from the computerized images of Paul's head.

The CT revealed a softball-size mass at the base of Paul's skull. It was invading brain tissue, extending into the muscles in the back of his neck, and eating away at bone. Most certainly it was malignant. The room that contained the CT scanner was separated from the control room by a large glass window, and through it, Paul could see an impressive number of white-coated figures huddled around computer monitors, craning their necks for glimpses of the mystery within. He took comfort in that. Imagine, so many people there just to serve him. Paul would be spared the realization that curiosity can look a lot like altruism when you are an interesting case.

Paul and his wife were informed that "a something" was seen on his scan that would need further study before he could be told what was causing his problems and how they could be treated. He was admitted to a private room, a spacious and well-furnished room that could have passed as hotel accommodations. The room offered a spectacular view, high above the city, and it seemed to Paul that he was assigned a space a little closer to God than most.

Morning hospital rounds amused Paul to no end. A sharp knock on the door would signal that the show was about to begin. It was not a knock of permission or of greeting, but one of announcement, heralding that something special was about to happen. The attending physician, clad in a sports coat, would enter first. It occurred to Paul that he was the ringmaster, and he was closely followed by an entourage of residents clad in long white coats, followed next by interns and medical students wearing short white coats. The nurses and pharmacists meekly brought up the end, filling the hospital room to capacity. It would be a standing-room-only performance.

The hushed room hung on the attending's every word, and Paul wondered if he was the only one who heard nothing in those words. Paul would hear that his something was still a something, but that tests were getting closer to providing information that could be discussed with him and his family. More tests would be scheduled to confirm the earlier tests. Paul was advised not to sweat the details, to let his doctors do the worrying, and was reassured that he was doing great. With the sharpness of a military drill team, sports coat, long coats, and short coats left the room as they had found it—in darkness, full of uncertainty and questions.

It wasn't until the evening of his fourth day in the hospital that some of Paul's questions were answered. It was late, well past the evening news, when a tall, serious-looking man in a white coat seemed to step out of the shadows and up to Paul's bedside.

"Mr. Prescot," the stranger started, "I'm Dr. Mass. I'm a cancer specialist and your doctors wanted me to talk to you about your cancer."

"I didn't know I had cancer," Paul responded with surprise.

"Yes, the biopsy three days ago confirmed it," Dr. Mass explained.

"I didn't know that I'd had a biopsy," Paul commented. Part of him wondered if this was all a mistake, but part of him had known, or at least suspected the truth for a couple of days. He wondered which part of himself would have to tell his wife.

The biopsy of the mass found on the CT scan had revealed squamous cell cancer, the same type as the skin cancer that had been removed the year before. It appeared that the unlikely had happened, that the small, easily treated skin cancer had spread into a very large problem. Paul would require extensive surgery to remove the tumor from his brain and the tissues of his neck. He was transferred to the neurosurgical service, and was never again to see the physicians who had admitted him. He would have liked to have said goodbye and thanked them for their care.

Paul discovered that neurosurgeons talked even less than internists, and, unfortunately, not in any language that he understood. The realization that he didn't even understand their language when they wrote it on paper forced him to smile a bit when he read the surgical consent. He wasn't expected to understand; only to sign the paperwork. Trust, on the other hand, seemed to be easy for Paul to find. He knew nothing of the people who intended to operate on his brain, but found great comfort in the knowledge that theirs was a profession of service. They would take good care of him. Paul knew somehow that he would be all right, a knowledge that would be a powerful force in the days that followed.

Two teams of surgeons were enlisted in the battle with Paul's tumor. The neurosurgeons were responsible for everything within the skull and involving the spinal cord, clearly the most tedious and time-consuming task. The orthopedic surgeons would take care of everything else. Together, it took the two surgical teams ten hours to complete their work. They did a good job. Paul was sitting up in a chair the next day, and by the second day the physical therapist was helping him walk. He had some damage to the nerves supplying the muscles of his right arm and the right side of his face, but considering the size of the tumor, Paul had fared remarkably well. He was transferred to a rehabilitation hospital with the expectation of a full recovery.

Within a week, Paul was back at the teaching hospital. He had had a stroke. It was not a large stroke, but it certainly complicated his plans for recovery. The stroke involved the same side that had been weakened by his surgery. CT scans, MRIs, echocardiograms, and countless other tests that he knew nothing about failed to explain the reason for the stroke, but his doctors knew what to do about it. It was his third team of doctors at the teaching hospital in as many weeks, and he marveled at how the physicians with the skills he needed most would show up in his life at just the right time.

It was the therapists, however, who moved Paul the most. They healed with their touch and their hearts. It seemed that one was always at his side, urging him to work a little harder and to reach a little farther. He wanted to get better, if only to please them. And better he got, finally returning to his home six weeks after he last left it.

Nothing instills more fondness for home than being away from it, and Paul reveled in his reunion. Every creaking floorboard, the once-annoying buzz from the bathroom light fixture, the soft pile of the bedroom carpet against his feet, every waking moment was a reminder of how much of life can be taken for granted, a chance to embrace the ordinary and find it extraordinary. The path of recovery that would take Paul back to his work would never stray far from the hospital. Three days before his eagerly anticipated return to work, Paul awoke with crushing chest pain, unable to catch his breath. On the way to the hospital, resigned that he was having a heart attack, Paul found much comfort in the practiced confidence of the young paramedic who rode with him in the back of the ambulance. Even the startling wail of the siren couldn't shake his sense that his journey would not end on that day.

The emergency room was a hive of activity when they arrived, and Paul felt a little embarrassed at being wheeled past the crowd of people who had gathered to wait for care. He hoped that he would not be responsible for them waiting even longer. Paul had always found comfort in the familiar, like sitting at the same table at the neighborhood diner and following an identical path every day on his walks, but being placed in the same examination room for the third time was a little unnerving. It provided a strange sensation of déjà vu, along with the discomfort of knowing that much of what he was experiencing had indeed happened before. The methodical efficiency of the busy emergency room seemed a little colder than he had remembered before—care was delivered with almost machinelike precision, with little time for explanations or a gentle hand placed on a shoulder. Even with all the technology and marvels of modern medicine that Paul had witnessed over the past months, it was the power of touch and the wisdom of words that had touched him the most. It was almost magical.

Paul was again admitted to the teaching hospital, this time under the responsibility of the pulmonary doctors. He had not had a heart attack. Rather, his symptoms stemmed from a pulmonary embolism—a blood clot had broken loose from somewhere in his body and lodged in his lungs. What would have killed many people became no worse than a major inconvenience, an awareness that brought Paul comfort, and an understanding that he still had lessons to learn and work to do.

Paul was home a week later, this time on blood thinners to protect him from developing another clot, and with renewed determination to return to work. But it would be an elusive target; each time his prize was locked securely in his sights, a new challenge would appear that would take Paul back to the hospital. With each readmission, Paul's family grew more weary and discouraged, and Paul found it increasingly difficult to remain optimistic and upbeat in their presence.

The last hospitalization had been the worst. He was admitted to the infectious disease service at the teaching hospital, a horrible choice of name, thought Paul. His doctors called it bacteremia—bacteria in his bloodstream. Paul only knew that it had left him feeling sicker than he had ever felt before, with days of high fever and shaking chills. Paul's family would learn that a portion of his bowels had ruptured, spilling infection throughout his abdomen.

Ruptured bowel was normally treated surgically, but Paul was too ill to undergo the procedure. Instead, his hope lay in potent antibiotics and the skill of the intensive care team to support him until his body had a chance to heal. One by one, major organ systems failed and technology was pressed into service; a ventilator for his failing lungs, dialysis for his failing kidneys, and a pacemaker for his failing heart. Twice Paul went into cardiac arrest, and twice his doctors resuscitated him back from the other side. Each intervention would buy a little time, a seemingly insignificant period to those among the intensive care team who had become jaded by their constant immersion in the low energy of illness. But every hour won became more valuable than the one that came before it, and to those who would pause to consider it, the brevity of life now seemed most significant.

Hours became days, days became weeks, and somewhere, lost in the current of time, Paul got better. It took more than a month before his doctors would declare him well enough to leave the hospital, but even then, his body was much too weak to return directly home. He would spend a few weeks in rehabilitation first, and after many weeks of lying in bed, the thought of being worked to the point of collapse by a therapist sort of appealed to Paul. While the body was exhausted, the mind was fresh and sharp, well exercised through weeks of observing the workings of life around him. To the surprise of his doctors, and often to their horror, he remembered everything about his hospitalization, even those times when they had thought he was unresponsive. Paul didn't quite understand it, but he recognized it as a powerful gift that would help him on his journey.

I set the folder containing the discharge summaries and referral letters about Paul on my desk. It was quite a story. I had yet to meet the man and already his chart was thicker than those of many patients I had followed for years. I knew much about the patient that I would soon see, but nothing of the man, except for a feeling that he would be special.

Paul Prescot presented an imposing figure. At six-foot-five and 190 pounds, he dwarfed the furniture in the examination room. Still, it was obvious that he had lost weight, and I wondered how much more commanding his presence had appeared before his illness. His balding head made his unusually large ears appear even larger, and evoked a feeling of great wisdom collected over many a journey. His face was weathered and creased, a monument to years of perpetual happiness, and made him seem like he had a story to tell. He extended his hand with a smile so broad that even his ears seemed to participate in the greeting.

I stood lost for a few moments studying his features, my hand becoming lost within the expanse of his. I knew that face, but I was uncertain from where. Perhaps it was the grocery store, or maybe the post office. It was a face that could have belonged to a neighbor or friend rather than a stranger.

As if sensing my thoughts, his smile never waning, he said, "We must have met before. It's a small neighborhood and I've been around for a long time. That's good. We can start out already as friends."

I sat with Paul and his wife and reviewed with them what his chart had told me. He sat quietly looking down at the floor as I listed his encounters with doctors over the past year. Skin cancer, brain tumor, brain surgery, blood infections, pulmonary embolus, respiratory failure, perforated bowel, and months of rehabilitation.

"That's quite a list," I noted, "and there's still more."

"Yes, "Paul agreed without looking up, "God has been good to me."

"I beg your pardon?" I asked, convinced that I had heard him wrong.

Like a parent explaining a wonder of the world to a young child, Paul looked into my eyes and said, "The beauty of sunrise only comes after the darkest part of the night. Faith has always come easy for me. I've never really had doubt, but then again, I had never faced such challenges before. We take so much for granted. I'm grateful for the opportunity to savor feeling good, to witness the healing power of love and friendship, and to feel my faith at work. It is very comforting."

After that first meeting, I seemed to run into Paul everywhere I went: the grocery store, the bakery, the bank. Invariably he was lost in conversation. The neighborhood hardware store seemed to be his particular favorite haunt. He was there so frequently that he was often confused for an employee.

One afternoon, I stopped into the barbershop not far from my home, desperate for a haircut. There is always a long wait for the single barber, so I tend to put off haircuts far too long. As was usually the case, the shop was packed, but in the midst of a half-dozen or so men sat Paul, holding court. He had the place howling with laughter with one story after another. The irony of a bald man sitting in a barbershop seemed to be lost on everyone, but as I watched Paul work his audience I couldn't think of a better place for him to be.

Driving home from the hospital one Saturday morning I saw Paul in a yard struggling with a wheelbarrow full of bricks. I pulled over in front of a church and walked back to the adjacent lot to see if I could help. Though he claimed he didn't need any help, nonetheless he accepted my assistance in moving his load to a tree ring in his yard that he was repairing. Of course, he had a story to tell me, actually two or three, which stretched a two-minute task into a quarter hour. Walking back to my car I couldn't help but notice that the architecture of Paul's home matched that of the neighboring church. I had driven by that church and its strategically placed illuminated sign thousands of times, but never paid it much attention. Today, I was intrigued by it. The sign welcomed visitors, announced Sunday's sermon, and listed the times of church school and worship services. Across the bottom was inscribed *Paul E. Prescot, Pastor*.

It would be a couple of weeks until I would see Paul again, when he came to the office for his routine visit. I had been seeing him every month or two for the better part of a year by that point. He stood as I walked into the room and extended his hand, his face turning into his signature smile.

"So, it's Reverend Prescot," I observed.

Looking a little embarrassed, he said, "No, it's Paul. If you must, Pastor Paul."

"But why?" I inquired.

With the sincerity of a close friend and the innocence of a child he offered an explanation. "Because I'm not sure that I am reverend, at least, not any more than anyone else. There is a part of me that's reverend, just as there is in you. It's not something that is proclaimed or that ordination bestows. It's something that is always with us, always has been, and always will, but we spend our lives and seldom recognize it."

I learned that Paul had been preaching for thirty years, twenty-five of them at the small church next door to him. I asked him if being ill had made his work difficult. I suspected that it had, but also suspected that he would never admit to it. His response not only surprised me, but opened my mind to possibilities that seemed far greater than anything I had considered before.

"Actually," Paul started out, "my work has never been easier. It's not work at all. I used to spend days preparing every sermon, researching scripture, and agonizing over the perfect words. Now, I have no idea what I am going to say when I stand up to speak, but I know that just the right words will be there. And they always are. I've always known about spirituality, but since those days spent in the silence of illness, a part of me knows *of* spirituality. All I have to do is get out of the way and let that part work."

As Paul spoke, I could picture him at work behind the pulpit at his church. It was something that I would like to see. But I had already seen Paul working—at the grocery store, in the barber shop, and standing in his front yard. He made people feel good about themselves, and in the process, he taught them how to feel good about others.

Paul was a subtle teacher. The levity of his jokes and the drama of his stories penetrated deep into the consciousness, retreating only after a small seed of wisdom had been planted. Most would be oblivious to the teaching at first, but in time, that seed would grow.

Several weeks would pass before I saw Paul again, when his wife rushed him to the office for back pain. Despite his protests that he was feeling fine, he walked stiffly and with slow, measured steps. His pain had started several days earlier, shortly after helping a neighbor move a refrigerator. Over-the-counter pain medication wasn't helping much, and other than making him smell like a cough drop, the muscle cream his wife had been rubbing on him didn't do much of anything. Paul was diagnosed with muscle strain and left the office with anti-inflammatory medication, muscle relaxants, and recommendations for hot soaks. When the pain hadn't improved after several days, a narcotic pain medication was added, although it took a lot of encouragement to get Paul to actually take it.

I expected Paul to be better in a week, but he wasn't. While the pain medication helped, it sedated him to a degree that was almost worse than the discomfort. He could work with pain, but feeling too tired to work was hard for him to accept. X-rays of his back didn't reveal any surprises, and Paul was enrolled in physical therapy. As days stretched to weeks, it was difficult to see much improvement.

Early one morning, Paul turned up in the emergency department at the local hospital. His wife found him too weak to get out of bed, and she called for an ambulance. By the time I made it in to the hospital, Paul's blood had been drawn, X-rays had been taken, and the results were posted on the chart that I would take to his bedside. So too was the explanation for his weakness.

I struggled not to show my surprise when I saw Paul. Although only a couple of weeks had passed since I had last seen him in the office, he appeared frail and weak, like an old man. His voice was thin and soft and his face drawn, but his smile was still radiant and reflected the feeling of peace that I had come to expect in his presence. I explained to Paul and his wife that every test that the emergency department had performed was normal, except one. His blood calcium level was markedly elevated, a level that would make him feel very tired and weak. It was something that we could treat.

"After all of the tests they did, if only one is abnormal, why do you look so worried?" Paul asked me.

"Well, because I don't know why the level is so high, but we need to find out," I explained. He nodded in understanding, but I had the feeling that the understanding came not from anything that I had said, but from what he had seen by peering into my soul. It made me feel a little uncomfortable at first, until he smiled again and I was left with a sense of gratitude.

When Paul's wife excused herself to telephone the family, he quietly said, "Thank you for not telling her. Not until you're sure."

I made arrangements to transfer Paul to the teaching hospital. Not many things could cause blood calcium to rise so high, but cancer was one of them. Squamous cell cancer was particularly infamous for such behavior, and I was concerned that his disease had recurred. His back pain suddenly took on greater significance, and I wanted Paul close to my specialists if my suspicions turned out to be true.

His stay at the teaching hospital would not produce good news. While his calcium level responded to treatment, his back pain worsened. MRI studies of Paul's back revealed extensive tumor involvement and a spinal tap showed that cancer cells had invaded his nervous system. Other imaging suggested that the cancer had also spread to his lungs and liver.

When Paul was admitted, a third-year medical student was assigned to his case. The student bubbled with excitement over the opportunity to observe what most of his classmates could only read about. He followed every laboratory result, studied every medication ordered, and performed detailed physical examinations to look for the slightest change.

On the evening that I told Paul the results of the studies, his medical student stood by my side. Paul never diverted his eyes from mine when I talked to him. When I told him that his cancer had returned and that the options for treatment were few, those eyes filled with tears.

Paul reached out for my hand and gently said, "I feel so bad for you."

"Why do you feel bad for me?" I asked in surprise, now my own eyes becoming a little misty.

"Because you have to tell people such horrible things. It must be so very hard on you," he said.

He paused for a few moments, smiled broadly, and continued, "You see, no matter what happens, I can't lose. If I live, I get to go home and spend more time with my family who loves me. If I die, I know where I'm going. I've always known, but it was in this very hospital room that I was able to see that other place. And it's good. No matter what happens to me in this place, the journey is just beginning. And that's good."

As I left Paul's room, I noticed his medical student sitting in an alcove at the end of the hall. I had forgotten all about him. I felt a little bad, as I had never noticed him leave, and frankly, never missed him. I walked towards him and could tell that he was crying, his shoulders heaving in rhythm with loud sobbing. I sat down next to him and waited, much as that old fire chief had done for me so many years earlier. Eventually, he looked at me through bloodshot eyes and shared his pain.

"You told him he was dying, but he was only concerned about you," he said in a voice of disbelief. "How can I become a doctor? I'm supposed to be here for him, but all I can think about is myself. I guess I've missed the whole point."

I placed my hand softly on his shoulder and said, "No, you got it. You are here to learn, but what they never tell you is that the learning never ends. We spend most of our careers learning—from books, journals, conferences. But the important things we learn from our patients. You will learn something from every patient that you encounter, but Paul is someone special. He has a way of turning our thoughts inward, helping us discover that the truly important lessons are those that we carry deep within.

"You will never forget Paul. You will never forget what you learned tonight, what you discovered. And that discovery will help shape the care you extend to every patient who comes your way. The pain you are feeling now will pass. It will be replaced by fond memories of a special man, and the lessons he helped you learn."

Together, we sat in silence, exploring the wisdom that could be found there.

CHAPTER 8

Dying Was the Best Thing That Ever Happened to Me

While I thought that I was learning how to live,
I have been learning how to die.
LEONARDO DA VINCI

Y ou didn't have to be a mover and shaker, a politician, a captain of industry, a government official, or on the social registry to recognize the name and face of Alexander Kipton, but certainly it would be those individuals who would know him the best. I was none of those things, but I recognized him instantly when I arrived for work one morning early in my career to find him sitting in my waiting room. It was hard to pick up a newspaper or turn on the evening news without seeing his face.

Alexander Kipton was the director of a prestigious consulting firm and a favorite son of the community. Everybody who was anybody wanted to know his opinion on the issues of the day and receive his blessing for their favorite projects. His favor could launch a political career, but if he withheld his support it could cause one to stall. He was advisor to the local parish priest and royal families from abroad. His participation in fundraising campaigns guaranteed success. His name was synonymous with power, influence, and accomplishment.

I had never met a famous person before, and I couldn't help but feel a shiver of excitement at his presence. I wasn't convinced that he hadn't mistakenly come to the wrong office, at least until he was ushered back to an examination room. Perhaps I was mistaken, and he simply had an uncanny resemblance to the man I only knew from pictures. I nervously shuffled through the registration papers in the chart that hung outside the closed examination room door. Sure enough, the man waiting on the other side of the door was Alexander Kipton.

I stood outside that door feeling strangely anxious. It was a sensation that I had had before, and my thoughts took me back to an earlier time, waiting outside the dean's office at my medical school, nervously awaiting the interview that would lead to my admission to the medical profession. Now, like then, making a good impression seemed to be of paramount importance. It was an idea that bothered me.

First impressions can be an invaluable tool in medicine, one that I often discounted during my early years in practice, finding comfort instead with the objectivity of clinical exams and diagnostic studies. But I've learned that the art of medicine is in the subjective, looking between the facts and figures, beneath the surface of the outer shell that we spend a lifetime building, and trusting the voice that we hear there. It is in those first few minutes with a new patient that I often hear that voice with the greatest clarity, unobstructed by personal history, unprejudiced by clinical findings, and unhindered by expectations.

My first impression of Alexander Kipton was of a person who liked to be in control, or who was at least accustomed to being in control. When I entered the exam room he stood, offered his hand, and said, "Bill, glad to meet you. You can call me Alex. Please, have a seat."

I didn't hesitate a moment. I sat and let him continue. It struck me, though, as an unusual role reversal. I had spent years perfecting the medical interview, learning how and when to ask just the right question, the question that would glean the most valuable information from even the most reluctant patients. Now those questions were being asked, and answered, by the patient. He presented a detailed and organized medical history, and did it better than most physicians could have. I wondered how long he had practiced.

It was clear that Alex didn't believe much in health maintenance and disease prevention. Time was too precious to be squandered in such a way. Seeking out a physician seemed justified only for a specific problem, and then, only after his efforts to solve the problem on his own had failed. Such was the purpose behind this visit.

Alex had been experiencing abdominal discomfort for many weeks. He described it as a burning pain in the upper abdomen, frequently moving up behind his breastbone to his throat. When it was severe, he even had a bitter taste in his mouth. He had considered the possibility of an ulcer, but discounted that when antacids didn't help much, and when he noticed that the pain was worse when he lay down to sleep at night. Acid-reducing medication helped him the most, but the relief did not last for the entire day. His self-diagnosis was gastroesophageal reflux, for which he needed acid-blocking medications.

It was a presentation that a medical student could be proud of; organized, logical, and most likely, accurate. I smiled at him and said, "Well, you certainly have made this easy. Why do you need me?"

Alex smiled back and stated the obvious. "I can't write a prescription. I need your medical license."

He permitted me the ritual of listening to his heart and lungs, feeling his abdomen, and checking his blood pressure. He patiently allowed me to fill in the gaps in his medical history, although they were remarkably few. He even endured the recommendations for cancer screening and health maintenance that I give all of my middle-aged male patients.

I wrote a prescription for a proton pump inhibitor, a medication routinely used for reflux. As I handed it to him, I looked him in the eye and asked, "Why me, Mr. Kipton? You must know any number of docs who would be thrilled to have you as a patient."

If he was surprised by my question, he didn't show it. In fact, I thought that I detected the hint of a smile with his reply. "Because I wanted the best, not someone who thinks that he's the best. And because my friend Karl Mannfeld trusted you, not only with his life, but with his death. He called you friend, and that makes you special."

The mention of Karl brought a catch to my throat. This would be the common ground that would help us build a relationship, but not on that day. As Alex left, I wondered what the real reason for his visit might have been. We teach the medical students that 60 percent of patients seeking care with a primary care physician do so for a psychosocial reason, regardless of what they might tell us. It was a statistic that always gave me pause, and one that I tried to keep active in my thoughts. I often wondered how many people had left my office in need. I had a strong sense that Alex was one of them.

A few days later, I sat waiting in an airport terminal for a flight that would take me home from a medical conference that I had attended. The flight was delayed, and there was little to do except read the newspaper and watch the news channel on one of the many televisions suspended from the ceiling. It was an election year and it was hard to escape the endless political commentary that starts earlier every election cycle. The media were masters at seeking out and exploiting dissent, if not conspirators to its creation. The newspaper reported on the advances made by the right, whereas the television provided radiant images of the left. It was a noxious brew, certain to offer most everyone something to which they could find offense. It was intoxicating, virtue and ideals subliminally eroded by the waves of low energy.

Between the announcements of flights boarding, flights arriving, and more flights delayed, I sat passively while an endless parade of talking heads flashed across the television screens, each telling their audience how they should be thinking, and why. One expert seemed no different than the one that came before or the one that would follow. It was almost hypnotic, until a flash of recognition snapped me into alertness. It was a face that I knew. Alex Kipton was being interviewed on national television.

I felt a surge of self-importance. Not only was someone from my community on television, but it was someone that I knew. The news anchor was interviewing Alex about the effects of negative campaign ads. He demanded to know why politicians seemed to be using more negative ads than ever before.

"Because they work," Alex observed calmly. "And because they know that the media will pick up on negative messages and play them over and over. That's a lot of name exposure that they don't have to pay for. It's not that I think positive messages won't work, it's just that you guys only seem to want to talk about the bad stuff. Journalism is at risk of moving away from reporting the news, to influencing the news."

The criticism appeared to sail over the head of the news anchor. Not batting an eye, he went on with the next question on his script. But I saw something revealing in the exchange. The Alex that I was watching on television appeared different than the Alex that sat in my office. This one was relaxed, smiled easily, and seemed concerned about the message that he projected and for those that would hear it. I wondered which Alex was the real thing.

It would be many months before I would see Alex in the office again. It took the persistence of a strong-willed wife to accomplish the task, or perhaps it was a simple strategy to silence debate about his health. His wife was a nurse and would occasionally check his blood pressure at home. With each measurement she became increasingly concerned, which irritated Alex to no end. He felt fine, and that should have been the end of the discussion.

I didn't tell Alex that I had seen him on television. In fact, I must have seen him on television a half-dozen times since that night at the airport. I wanted his visits to be about him, and not me. I wanted him to feel sanctuary in my office, far from the routine he experienced every day. But nonetheless, I was fascinated by the man who sat before me, and the disparity between him and the image that I had grown accustomed to on television.

At first glance, and even after second and third looks, the person Alex appeared identical to the image Alex. But there were striking differences. The Alex on television consistently projected comfort, at home in front of cameras and under the scrutiny of questions. The person Alex never seemed comfortable in the office. That was far from unusual, though. Many people seem alienated when on the physician's turf, but somehow, I just couldn't see anything, or anyone, giving Alex Kipton pause.

Alex was the consummate gentleman—respectful, polite, and with behavior that was the definition of proper. His body language exuded self-confidence. Our meetings always seemed more appropriate to the boardroom than the examination room.

It was hard to look at Alex Kipton and not see success. He was at the pinnacle of his career. Achievement had become so routine, so expected, that it had become a foregone conclusion. I had always thought that this was the secret to happiness, and if so, Alex Kipton should have been the poster child for happiness. But as we talked about his blood pressure that day in the office, I started to have my doubts.

Alex grudgingly acknowledged that his blood pressure had been trending up over the past year, a concession to the data that lay plotted on a graph before him. He viewed it as a personal defeat, one that could only be mitigated by correcting the problem on his own. He would lose a little weight, eat better, and exercise more. Taking medication was out of the question.

"How stressful is your life, Alex?" I asked him.

"Stress is good for you," he replied. "It keeps us motivated and heading in the right direction. When we feel a little stress we produce our best, and it makes success taste all the more sweet."

Alex hated questions about himself, but I wasn't about to be deterred this time. "But you didn't answer the question. How stressful is your life?"

"Probably a lot less than most people's," he said with a slight edge of defensiveness in his voice. "I think most stress comes from not accomplishing what you set out to do. And I make a point of doing just that. You don't have stress when you know the outcome of each day before it starts. But I don't know what any of this has to do with the price of beans," he demanded, now clearly irritated.

"Well, it's like this, Alex," I responded in a soft voice, as if trying to soothe a resting giant that I had started to anger. "You first came to me with indigestion and reflux, probably more severe than you admitted. Although you minimize it, you often complain of back and neck pain. And now your blood pressure is up. All of these things can be influenced by stress. Docs can throw medications at problems, and perhaps treat symptoms, but if we miss the underlying problem, nothing is truly accomplished."

"You are right, of course," he said, obviously embarrassed. He was silent for a few moments, smiled, and continued. "Actually, I do feel stress. Every time I come here."

I returned his smile with a bit of a revelation. That disparity I felt between the man on television and the one who sat before me was exemplified by that smile. Relaxed and fluid in photographs and on television, his smile was stiff and forced in person, almost as if it had been practiced from an instruction manual.

Images of a clinic patient that I used to care for during my residency formed in my thoughts. It was strange that I would think of her at that particular moment. When meeting a new doctor she would sit quietly and stare intently into the face of her physician. When asked about the behavior, she would reply that she was looking for a smile. A smile, she explained, was a window into a person's soul. Happy souls smiled.

"Are you happy, Alex?" It was a question that I had been mulling over in my mind, and I was almost as surprised as Alex that I'd asked it out loud.

Startled, Alex responded, "Anything that I want, I have, or can go out and get. Of course I'm happy."

"You seem uncomfortable with the question," I noted, feeling a little uncomfortable myself.

"No, not at all," he assured me. "It's just that Karl asked me that very question the last time I saw him, the same day that he gave me your name and urged me to contact you."

"Sometimes," I reflected, "why a question is asked is just as important, or more so, than the answer."

Months turned into years, and Alex's visits remained rare occasions. His stoic nature made it difficult for him to complain, and when he called, I knew the reason was important. Though his blood pressure was often borderline, stress was never to be discussed again. But I would often wonder about his happiness, and at times, even considered the possibility that he might be depressed.

Five or six years after I first met Alex, he began experiencing strange sensations in his chest. Typically he would ignore such things, and the cold symptoms or aches and pains would always pass within a few days' time. When the chest sensations didn't go away, he began considering the possible causes. Such preoccupation disturbed Alex. It was wasted energy. The vague nature of the distress also bothered Alex, as he considered himself a skilled observer and communicator. But descriptors eluded him. It wasn't pain, pressure, or any of the other symptoms that he had read about that could signal heart disease. As unsatisfying as it was, he only knew that it was there, and that it was a presence that hadn't been there before.

Alex suspected that his acid reflux was bothering him again, a hypothesis that he tested with antacids. Sure enough, he felt better after taking them. While he denied any concerns to his family, it was hard to hide the roll of antacids that he always had within reach. He dismissed his wife's urging to call me. After all, he knew what the problem was and how to manage it.

One crisp winter morning found Alex sitting in a meeting with community leaders, discussing a charity drive that he had been asked to spearhead. It was a meeting no different than any of the others that filled his life. Even the open roll of antacids that sat on the table in front of Alex had been a fixture for many weeks. Toward the end of the meeting, Alex felt the now-familiar sensation in his chest. It was the same as all of the other times, and he reflexively reached for his antacids. But this time, Alex did something that he had never done before. He got up and left his meeting, early.

Alex drove across town to the teaching hospital and found a place to park in the parking garage. With antacids in hand, he made his way to the emergency department and waited patiently in line to be registered. As he stood before the harried registration clerk, he calmly placed his hand to his chest and told her, "I think something is wrong with my heart."

Slumping across the terrified woman's desk, striking his head on the way down, Alex promptly died.

The emergency department had a sophisticated communication system to alert the nursing and medical staff of the type and severity of problems presenting to the reception area. It wasn't needed for Alex. The screams from the clerk were sufficient. The charge nurse was the first to Alex's side, quickly determined that he was breathless and without a pulse. They started CPR and Alex was moved to a trauma room. If a miracle was to happen, it would happen there.

Except for brief moments, the emergency department was a place of chaos. Alex represented one of those moments when the chaos coalesced into choreography. Technicians, nurses, respiratory therapists and physicians united around Alex in a well-rehearsed dance. Intravenous lines were started while electrodes were placed on his chest to attach him to the cardiac monitor. The monitor revealed ventricular fibrillation. Electrical defibrillator paddles were placed on his chest and discharged, but the rhythm of Alex's heart remained that of death. After three attempts to shock his heart into compliance had failed, the body of Alex Kipton was taken over by medical science. A tube was passed into his airway and he was connected to a ventilator. A machine would now breathe for him. Hands compressing his breastbone would circulate the blood throughout Alex's body, and the worried doctors that hovered around his bed would think for him. Medications were infused to stabilize his heart, and he was shocked with electricity again. This time, his heart rhythm returned to normal. From death to life—in a mere ten minutes.

A heart attack was the most likely cause of Alex's cardiac arrest, but it would take time for laboratory tests to prove, time that could alter his chance for survival. Alex was immediately taken to the cardiac catheterization laboratory. If he had had a heart attack, a blocked coronary artery could be opened with angioplasty.

By the time I made it to the hospital, Alex had been moved to the intensive care unit. Three men in suits spoke in hushed tones not far from his room, one of whom I recognized as the mayor. It seemed in keeping with Alex's priorities that the mayor would beat his physician to the hospital.

Alex was still on the ventilator when I entered his room, and heavily sedated. The monitor revealed a normal cardiac rhythm, normal blood pressure, and a normal level of oxygen in his bloodstream. Sterile gauze had been placed over a laceration on his forehead. It was a large laceration, and bone was visible at its base. Drugs to stabilize abnormal heart rhythms hung from a pole beside his bed and slowly dripped into his veins.

The results of the cardiac catheterization were both reassuring and confusing. The coronary arteries revealed no blockages;

Alex had not had a heart attack. The heart muscle appeared healthy and moved as a normal heart would be expected to. The echocardiogram and laboratory studies were also normal. Alex had experienced sudden death, but there was no explanation as to why. One thing was certain, however. If he hadn't been standing in the emergency department when it had happened, he probably never would have survived.

Alex came off the ventilator without any difficulties later that day. The plastic surgeons closed the wound on his forehead. By the second hospital day, he was walking around his room, a bit confused about all that had happened to him, and even more confused at the fuss that everyone made over him. He had many visitors, but uncharacteristically he had little to say, electing to listen instead.

The cause of his cardiac arrest could only be guessed at, but it was an educated guess. Those strange sensations that he thought were reflux were probably episodes of irregularity in his heart rhythm. Sometimes irregularity in the rhythm can be deadly. Without knowing why it had happened, however, it would be difficult to prevent it from happening again.

A specialist in the electrical activity of the heart was asked to see Alex. He recommended an implantable defibrillator. Similar to a pacemaker, the unit would be implanted beneath the skin on the chest wall, with electrodes passed through a large vein in the shoulder to the heart. The device would monitor the heart continuously, and if a life-threatening rhythm was detected, a small electrical charge would be delivered directly to the heart, much as was done when Alex was in the emergency department. It could be lifesaving should another such event occur.

When faced with this proposal, I expected Alex to howl in protest. After all, this was the man I had spent the better part of a year trying to get to take medication for his blood pressure. This was the man who believed cholesterol and cancer screening were important, only for other men. So I was both elated and surprised when he looked at the cardiologist and calmly stated, "Fine. You're the expert and you know what's best." Three days after experiencing clinical death, Alex walked out of the hospital, without the help of a wheelchair, but with an implantable defibrillator.

Several weeks later I saw Alex in the office for a follow-up appointment. As was his custom, he had requested the morning's first appointment. He had figured, quite accurately, that the first appointment of the day would be the one most likely to start on time, immune from the unexpected but inevitable delays encountered throughout the patient-care day. And as usual, he beat me to the office and was already sitting in the waiting room when I walked through.

As I walked by, he looked up and smiled. I thought the smile seemed warmer than usual. It was a fleeting thought, quickly consumed in the frenzied moments that open every day in the office. Thumbing through a stack of telephone messages for items of urgency, I couldn't help but take notice of Alex's conversation with the office staff as they were checking him in. He paused to comment on how happy they seemed, and to inquire about their families. It was atypical of Alex. He had always been all business on his previous visits, never squandering time or words that did not further his purpose for being there.

Alex was standing when I walked into the examination room, intently inspecting a photograph of a pied-billed grebe that hung on the wall. He didn't seem to notice my presence until he heard the door close. He slowly turned and smiled at me. Indeed, the smile was different. It had warmth and spontaneity. It was the smile that I had noticed in photographs and on television, but had never encountered in person. It was a smile that had energy to it, energy that reached out to touch you. It brought a smile to my face. It made me feel happy, as did the realization that I was looking at a happy man.

"Dying was the best thing that ever happened to me," Alex proclaimed in an uncharacteristic booming voice.

They were powerful words and not what I was expecting. They touched the very fiber of my existence. They were saturated with wisdom, wisdom that seemed beyond the capability of man, wisdom that seemed to be from another place. I tingled with anticipation as I sat down in a chair facing Alex. I had a feeling that something very special was about to happen.

"Tell me about it, Alex," I said, unable to keep the excitement out of my voice. "What happened to you?"

"I understand everything," he said, with a tinge of awe in his voice. "I know why I am here, where I'm going, and what I should be doing along the way. I woke up in the hospital with a feeling of contentment that I had never known before, or even thought possible. The feeling hasn't left me."

"I never gave much thought to death. It was something that happened to others—the old, the careless, the stupid, or just the plain unlucky. I was never any of those things. I would read about it every day and see it on television; like the teenager killed in the car accident yesterday, or that man that died last week from carbon monoxide poisoning in his basement workshop. Ordinary people doing ordinary things. The thought never crossed my mind that it would happen to me. Our intellect knows that everything will die, but our ego tries hard to keep such truths away from our thoughts."

"Do you remember anything that happened to you?" I asked.

His smile broadened a bit as he asked, "You mean, do I remember walking towards a bright light? Everyone asks me that, but no, there wasn't any light. At least, I didn't think so at the time."

"You don't sound too sure of yourself, Alex," I noted.

"Well, I'm not. I've been spending a lot of time alone the past couple of weeks. Quiet used to drive me nuts. The television was always tuned to a news channel. The radio was always on in the car. I would fall asleep at night to music, and awake in the morning with more music. But now, I find myself looking for quiet places. I savor silence. Imagine me, sitting alone in the woods, taking pleasure in the stillness.

"Somewhere in that stillness came understanding. It was as if a light turned on in a dark room. So if understanding is light, well then, maybe I did walk into the light."

"Just what do you understand, Alex?"

He looked at me as if the answer was too simple for words. "Now," he said. "It's all about now."

He let his words sink in for a few moments before continuing. "I've spent my career, most of my life, in fact, looking forward. I've convinced others that purpose can be found in their futures, but only if they understand and take advantage of their pasts. But life happens now, and it can be lost in yesterday, or misspent waiting for tomorrow.

"I used to take comfort in my plans for the future. Regardless of whether I ever acted on those plans, they were always there, waiting with infinite patience. It made me immortal. But death was very liberating. I saw the past for what it is; a mere shadow on the trail giving witness that someone has passed that way. As for tomorrow, it became so apparent that it is just an illusion, a very powerful and seductive one. The epiphany lives in what's left over, and the realization that now, this very moment, is truly infinite. It will always be now. And if we can learn to always live in the present moment, we achieve immortality. There is nothing that we cannot experience, nothing that we cannot accomplish."

I was deeply moved by his words. It would take some time before I would fully grasp their meaning, and start to explore their potential in daily life. But I knew they were special and worthy of understanding. Just watching Alex told me that. I could feel the happiness, the peace within him.

"Alex," I observed, "I don't think I've ever seen you this happy before."

"Well, that's just the way I feel. I can't stop smiling. It's strange," he went on. "I've taught hundreds of people how to look happy. It never occurred to me that the easiest way to look happy is to be happy."

Alex stood up and walked over to another photograph hanging on the wall, this one of a little blue heron. "Strange," he noted, half thinking out loud. "Of all the times I've been here, I never noticed these before. Karl asked me what I thought of them."

Tapping the glass covering the photograph, he looked back at me and asked, "How long did you have to wait before you took this picture?"

"I'm not quite sure," I replied, "certainly a number of hours."

"The peace and quiet must be wonderful," he noted wistfully. "You must find a lot of wisdom in that stillness."

"Well, I know that I like it and I feel at peace when I'm out with a camera. I guess there is a wisdom in that. But wait a minute, how could Karl have asked you about the pictures? He died before you started coming here."

Alex thought about it for a moment, shrugged his shoulders, and smiled. "I'm not so sure he did."

With that, he turned and walked out of the office. I would learn later that Alex had quit his job. After a few months away from the pubic eye, he would take his talents to the classroom, much to the delight of the local university. I could think of no greater way to serve. His career and experience would be a vast resource, but it would be that day he spent in the emergency room that would help open minds to new possibilities and the timelessness of now.

CHAPTER 9

The Wisdom of Medicine

Knowledge comes, but wisdom lingers.
ALFRED LORD TENNYSON

Wisdom begins in wonder.
SOCRATES

It is amazing how much thinking can be done in an elevator, particularly the elevators at the teaching hospital. In the time it takes to travel from the ground floor to the medical floor, Einstein could have furthered his theories of relativity and quantum mechanics. Too few elevators and too great a demand nourished impressive crowds within the lobby, crowds of people atypically patient, or perhaps deadened with resignation. It was the slowest part of my commute, one that seemed to get longer with each passing year.

Wedged into a corner of the elevator, I stood conspicuously protecting a box of doughnuts from a crushing fate. They were to be a peace offering for the medical team that awaited me many floors above, a tool of greeting and a reflection of my intention that the month to come would be a good one. Things hadn't changed all that much since the time that I waited in that room as a new resident. The surest, if not the fastest, way into a medical student's or resident's heart was to feed them.

As the door opened and closed, I was lost in thought. Visions of my first ride in that very same elevator played out in my mind. They were images with an uncommon, if not disturbing, clarity. They were images of a young man both excited and frightened by his new role as a resident physician—eager to serve, impatient to learn, and humbled by the responsibility that lay ahead.

Now, some two decades later, the responsibility that awaited still humbled me. For the next month, I would be the attending physician on a medical ward team. It would be a large team, made up of a student pharmacist, junior and senior medical students, several interns, and a supervising resident. For the next month, I would be responsible for their education, their professional development, their welfare, and the care that they would provide to their patients. The job had changed little over the years, and I had done it so many times that it had almost become routine. But I had changed, and the way that I practiced medicine had changed with me. While the way I taught had surely changed as well, at times I was aware of a soft voice from deep within me that suggested that, perhaps, I hadn't changed enough. Usually I heard that voice during times of quiet and reflection; I wasn't expecting to hear it so clearly in that crowded, noisy elevator.

Few professions savor tradition with more fervor than medicine. The Hippocratic oath is still recited at medical school graduations, and despite the technological advances, the training of new physicians has changed surprisingly little through the eons. Medical education is a very hierarchal system in which each level of experience, from medical student to attending physician, imparts knowledge to the ones below. With the flow of knowledge comes the love of and comfort with the status quo and the perpetuation of tradition.

To a medical student, the attending physician can assume godlike qualities, a role that the ego is not anxious to relinquish. The attending is always right. The awe and respect I held for my first attendings still quickens my pulse when I pass these professors, now emeritus, in the halls of the teaching hospital.

A bell announced the arrival of the elevator to each floor. I had never appreciated how similar the sound was to the old nursing call signals that once filled the air at the teaching hospital. The sound carried me back to my own internship, sitting in a conference room listening with astonished silence as my attending described his training. Interns' duty schedules had been so heavy that they lived at the hospital, on call in the wards every other night. Each intern was responsible for thirty or forty patients. When not on duty, they were expected to study, and each had memorized the *Physician's Desk Reference*, the compendium listing every medication that was available for physicians to prescribe. He was quick to point out that these were ordinary accomplishments, and that the only disadvantage of being on call every other night was that you missed out on half of the good cases. I was humbled by the giant who sat before us.

It would be a couple of years before the legendary giants who once roamed the hospital took on more mortal qualities for me. While it was true that our predecessors cared for entire wards of patients by themselves, it was a different age with different capabilities. Time was often the only treatment available. Pneumonia patients who now receive antibiotics at home once required hospitalization lasting weeks. Tuberculosis patients could spend a year in a hospital bed. Even childbirth would result in a week's admission.

In the years following the Korean War, the golden age of medicine when many of my teachers learned their trade, there were only some forty medications available for physicians to prescribe. Penicillin and sulfa were wonder drugs. Memorizing the *Physician's Desk Reference* didn't seem that great a feat with the perspective of time.

With time, I came to realize that it was just that lack of technology and the paucity of miraculous medications that made my teachers great doctors—and giants in fact. They diagnosed by observing and by listening. They treated by touching and by caring. They became more than physicians; they were healers.

Just as I practiced the science of medicine, my earliest days in academic medicine were spent teaching that science. I knew little else other than to teach as I had learned, perpetuating our traditions. Morning rounds at the teaching hospital were anchored by twenty or thirty minutes at the blackboard, lecturing on the pathophysiology and management of one of the myriad maladies that we encountered on the medical wards. Excellence in patient care was as much an academic pursuit as a caring one, and at times, the distinction was difficult for us to see.

Many of the people in the elevator were patients, no doubt, some arriving for early morning studies and procedures. They could have been my patients. I found myself looking into their faces, and in those eyes I could see fear, determination, courage, but most of all, uncertainty. To those who caught my eye, I smiled reassuringly. It was something that my patients had taught me to do, and judging from the reactions of my elevator companions, it worked equally well with perfect strangers. My patients had taught me a great deal. That realization seemed strangely appropriate as the elevator moved me ever closer to my ward team.

As I started my medical practice, it didn't take long for me to find the science of medicine lacking. It provided the basis of diagnosis and the fundamentals of treatment, but it never seemed to make a difference in the lives of my patients. My science helped cure, but it didn't heal. Healing I would learn with time, and I would learn it from my patients. It was the art of medicine that I had always heard about, but had never truly understood until the lives of my patients became an important part of my own life.

The faculty of a medical school is rich with ego, and no doubt mine rendered an overly generous assessment of my value to medical education. It didn't take long, however, to realize that the residents and medical students that I worked with were adults, not the children that they were often treated as. Even more heretical was the realization that I was unable to teach them medicine. The best that I could offer was to help them learn.

As my patients taught me how to be a doctor, I tried to help others learn medicine. Those early years of helping students learn the science of medicine were gradually replaced with the desire that they learn the art of medicine. It was something that I could not teach. They would learn just as I was learning, through the lives of our patients. Gathering around the patients' bedsides to demonstrate the findings from a physical exam became less important than taking time to talk and to learn about their lives. This is where the magic could be found, and the place from where the colors of the artist's brush flowed.

I would start each new ward month, on the very first day, with an observation from the French author Voltaire. "The art of medicine consists in amusing the patient while nature cures the disease." This was invariably met with indignation, albeit silent indignation—best to not challenge the new attending on the first day of the rotation. Surprisingly, it was the medical students who felt most threatened by the concept. Being in control was central to their efforts and dreams. The notion that patients could get better without them was somehow frightening. If it was a concept that they had never considered before, it would be one that most would be eager to forget. Those who would remember would become artists.

The longer I looked at those faces in that elevator, the more they reminded me of my patients, and not just any patients. They reminded me of those special souls, many of whom had long passed, who had written an indelible passage in my life story. They had each brought a morsel of wisdom, sometimes from the world about me that I was too busy to notice, but more often, from distant places that I knew little of. It was wisdom with the power to transform, creating those moments of awareness that one looks back upon as epiphanies on life's path. Strange that I would be visited by those ghosts in that elevator, but appropriately strange. Most doctors master the science of medicine. Some are accomplished practitioners of its art. Few are touched by its wisdom.

As the elevator doors opened onto the floor that would take me to my ward team, I felt an unaccustomed anticipation, one that I hadn't felt since my earliest days of attending, when the potential to make a difference was both a heavy burden and an exhilarating opportunity. There are occasional moments during the training years when circumstance, or a message, can be powerful enough to change the way one will practice medicine forever. It is a staggering power for a teacher. Your touch can extend beyond the student to every patient the student will ever care for. Somehow, science and art didn't seem to be enough. If only we could teach the wisdom of medicine.

It was always cold in the conference room where our team met daily for rounds. The air conditioning could never be turned off, even in the dead of winter. It provided perhaps the best use for the white coats that everyone wore: to keep warm. The continuous rush of air from the ventilation system competed with every conversation and every desire for a moment of quiet. It always seemed like a bad omen on that first day of each ward rotation. The team was miserable before I had a chance to utter a single word.

As was usually the case when I walked into that room, everyone sat huddled around the conference room table in their coats, some even wrapped in blankets from the linen room. As we waited for a few stragglers to arrive, I surveyed what was to become my new team. Most of the faces were new to me, and all appeared incredibly young. The fact that they seemed younger every year always served to remind me that time waits for nobody. Strangers now, soon we would know each other very well. We would know each other's strengths, weaknesses, and passions. I looked from face to face and couldn't help but notice their eyes.

I was fascinated with their eyes. They were more informative than the name tags pinned to their coats or the picture identification badges hanging from their pockets. I had become good at judging their level of training just by looking at them. The junior medical students were the easiest. Their eyes betrayed the terror that they felt. The senior medical students did a better job of hiding their fear, but the eyes couldn't keep the secret. The interns had tired eyes, eyes that always seemed to be in motion, no doubt visualizing the many tasks awaiting their attention. The eyes of the senior residents intrigued me the most. They exuded quiet confidence, but not the happiness one would expect from a young physician near-ing the end of training. Like a cataract clouding the lens of an older eye, responsibility dampened the sparkle that should have been there. It was the first time that many had experi-enced the burden of responsibility, accountable not only for their own decisions, but for those of the residents and stu-dents who worked under them.

The doughnuts were a huge success, as I had known they would be. If the first principle of medicine was to do no harm, then the second had to be that students and residents were always hungry. It didn't seem that long of a look back to my own years in training, and the vivid remembrance of the joy that a Danish could produce on morning rounds. It wasn't that they couldn't get their own breakfast, although medical students were perennially broke. There just always seemed to be something that was more important than eating.

As was typical on the first day, the team hung on my every word, not to glean what knowledge I might impart, but rather searching for clues that might predict their fortunes for the coming month. Patients admitted to the medicine service at the teaching hospital were distributed among four ward teams. Call, a twenty-four-hour period during which they would be assigned new patients who required hospital admission, rotated among the teams every four days. My team was not busy, as they were on call and would be receiving new admis-sions throughout the day and night. Already two patients were waiting for the senior resident to evaluate in the emergency room. We spent the morning talking about the patients we had inherited from the previous month's team. One man with chest pain, one with diverticulitis, an elderly lady with asthma, two patients with pneumonia, and the saddest case, Mrs. Ambert, a young mother of three children who had spent the last three years in a persistent vegetative state following a skiing accident. She lived in a nursing home and frequently needed to be admitted to the hospital for urinary tract infections. All in all, pretty standard fare on the internal medicine floors.

It was late in the day when I was surprised by a page from Allen Thomas, one of the fourth-year medical students on the team. Although I had given the team my telephone numbers earlier that day, and encouraged them not to hesitate to call me, it was rare for them to do so. Residents hated calling their attendings for help, many believing it a sign of weakness. The trick was to find a way to help them without making them feel like they had asked for it.

I had already decided that Allen was going to be interesting to watch. Of all the trainees that made up a ward team, it was the fourth-year medical students who could be the most unpredictable. Third-year students were typically too overwhelmed by the transition from classroom and theory to bedside medicine to offer many surprises. Responsibility kept the residents from showing much individuality, or, far too often, creativity. It was this burden of responsibility that the senior students lacked. They served as acting interns, managing patients like one of the interns, but under the close supervision of the senior resident. It was a wonderful opportunity to learn and to grow, before their lives changed forever and their signatures actually meant something.

During rounds earlier that day, I was amused by Allen's confidence as he presented his patients to me. It almost bordered on arrogance. He spoke as if he were a master of the medical literature and a beneficiary of vast experience. I had seen this before, an aliment that afflicted some medical students as they neared graduation, a surrendering to the ego now that their journey was near its end and the hard work was almost over. It never seemed to occur to them that the hard work was yet to come.

I returned Allen's call, recognizing the number as being from the emergency room. He asked for my help in discharging a patient who he and his resident believed did not require hospitalization. It was a belief that occurred to the residents with regularity, and conflict was common between medical residents and their emergency medicine colleagues. What wasn't common, however, was for the residents to challenge an admission and to bring their attending into the dispute.

Allen and his resident, Joseph Martelli, were waiting for me when I arrived in the emergency room. I had known Dr. Martelli since he was an intern and had always found his work exceptional. Judging by his reputation, the rest of the faculty agreed with me. He seemed rather embarrassed at my presence, and I think he would just as soon have admitted the patient and discussed the details with me in the morning. Allen was the one carrying the torch on this battle, convinced that the patient could be treated adequately and more easily as an outpatient.

The patient in the eye of the storm was Jeanne McClanahan, a forty-year-old woman traveling through town with her son. They were on their way to visit relatives in Michigan when car trouble forced them to pull off to the side of the interstate. The police officer who stopped to help them thought that Jeanne appeared ill and dropped her and her son off at the emergency room while he arranged to have the car towed. The emergency room physician felt that she needed to be hospitalized for pneumonia.

"Does this look like pneumonia to you?" Allen inquired with a voice loud enough to ensure that everyone in the department knew of our discussion. With the snap of his wrist he whipped the chest X-ray onto the viewbox. He must have practiced that maneuver for hours. I hadn't seen it done better by radiologists on television.

"Pretty bad pneumonia not to have a white count," he said, triumphantly handing me the laboratory reports.

I had to admit, the chest X-ray looked normal to me. Perhaps, if I used my imagination, I could detect a little fluffiness at the base of the left lung, but I wouldn't have put it in writing. There was no ambiguity with the laboratory studies. They were stone-cold normal. It appeared that Allen was right, but that realization irritated me, and I didn't know why.

When all else fails, physicians resort to examining patients in order to make a diagnosis. With Allen and Dr. Martelli in tow, I went to see Mrs. McClanahan. She wasn't what I expected and I glanced at her birth date on the chart to make sure I had the right patient. The forty-year-old lady before me looked closer to sixty. Her features were coarse, the thick wrinkled skin giving the impression that her face had been chiseled from wood. Her eyes were tired, and they suggested sadness. I wondered when she had last slept. Despite her distressed appearance, I liked this woman. It was as if we had met before.

Mrs. McClanahan was sitting up in bed. A dinner tray was sitting on the wheeled bed table in front of her. I introduced myself and asked permission to listen to her lungs, promising to take only a moment so that her food did not get cold.

"That's OK," she replied, looking over at her son. "I'm really not hungry and I don't think I can eat."

When I reached to push the table out of the way, she grabbed at her tray with a suddenness that startled me. I assured her that I wasn't going to take the tray, but after she tasted our food, she may wish I had. She laughed at my attempt at humor while I listened to her back and chest.

After my brief examination, I turned my attention to the son that sat quietly next to her bed. He looked to be about fifteen. He was tall and lanky, and had brilliant red hair that did not seem to have a close relationship with a comb. I learned that his name was James Thomas, although his family called him Tommy. It was the first time that he had ever seen the inside of a hospital. He wore a heavy, faded flannel shirt, which seemed odd, as the temperatures had been quite warm for the past week. His blue jeans were worn, beltless, and ended several inches before his legs did. He answered my casual questions politely, ending every reply with *sir*. But he seldom looked at me. His attention was reserved for his mother.

I stepped into the hall with Dr. Martelli and Allen to discuss Mrs. McClanahan. Allen beamed in delight, knowing that he had proved his case to the attending. I agreed that if she had pneumonia, it was very mild, or perhaps too early to show up on the X-ray. I routinely treated far sicker people in my office as outpatients. But something just didn't add up.

"Let's go ahead and admit her." I concluded. "We can always discharge her in the morning if things don't change."

Allen looked as if he had been shot. "You've got to be kidding?" he asked incredulously. "We are too busy taking care of people who really need to be here to waste our time like this."

"Look," I explained quietly, "we don't pick our patients, they select us. The ER doc saw something that concerned him, and we should give him the benefit of the doubt, step back a little, and maybe we will see the same thing by morning."

I reached for my wallet, pulled out a twenty, and handed it to Allen. "Now I want you to do me a favor," I went on. "Take Tommy to the cafeteria and buy him dinner. You eat too, it's my treat. Get him whatever he wants. When you're done, take him over to the gift shop and get him something to read for tonight."

Allen looked at me in stunned silence. "I'm a doctor, not a social worker," he finally commented softly, words that I don't think he intended anyone to hear.

"Actually, Allen," I observed, "you are a medical student, and much of medicine could be considered social work. You are going to find yourself a nurse, a pharmacist, a therapist, and even a chaplain before your days in medicine are over. One day, you are going to look in the mirror and find that you are whatever your patient needs. That's our job. That's what we do.

"Look, we clearly don't know the entire story here. Take a good look at Mrs. McClanahan. She doesn't appear to be the picture of health. Spend some time with her son. You may learn something that can be of help to her. You have an opportunity to help someone, perhaps even make a difference in someone's life. Not many people have that gift."

Allen looked thoughtful for a moment, and perhaps with understanding, or maybe with only a simple desire not to antagonize his boss, he slipped the money into his shirt pocket and disappeared into the McClanahan room. It was the start of an unexpected journey, a journey that would leave him forever changed.

The team was in good spirits the following morning when I arrived for rounds. They had completed their first night on call without incident and had enjoyed an unusually quiet night in the hospital. Allen stood in stark contrast to his colleagues. He seemed withdrawn and pensive and did not help himself to the bagels and orange juice that I had brought for breakfast. As his teammates presented their patients, Allen sat at the end of the table and listened quietly, but he was clearly in another place. We talked about a diabetic lady with a foot ulcer, a college student with asthma, an older man with gout, and how to manage a schoolteacher with a positive TB skin test. Finally, it was time to hear from Allen.

"Dr. Thomas," I said. "What's on your mind?"

It took a minute for him to answer, time that bred a sense of anticipation in the silence of the conference room. There was an almost reverent quality to Allen, sitting quietly with head bowed and hands folded in front of him.

"How did you know?" he asked softly without looking up.

"I'm sorry?" I asked, not at all sure that he had said anything.

Allen looked up at me with bloodshot eyes. He obviously hadn't slept, but I thought I saw more than fatigue in those eyes. "How did you know that he was hungry?" he asked again.

"I'm not sure that I did," I started to reply.

"Yes you did, sir." he interrupted, now with an edge of urgency in his voice, "Please, how did you know that Tommy was hungry?"

"Let's talk about it, Allen," I suggested. "But first, why don't you go ahead and present your patient to us."

"The workup I did yesterday doesn't seem relevant today," he replied in frustration.

"Well, why don't you tell us what your admitting impression was, and what has changed to make it all irrelevant today?" I asked.

Allen took a deep breath, sighed, and started his story.

"Jeanne Mae McClanahan is a forty-year-old lady without significant past medical history who was traveling through town with her son when they experienced car trouble. She was brought to the ER because of fever, cough, and symptoms of fatigue. Clinical examination was unremarkable, laboratory studies were normal, as was the chest X-ray and EKG. My clinical impression was that of a viral respiratory tract infection with fatigue exacerbated by travel. While she could have been managed as an outpatient, she was admitted for observation, to reevaluate this morning.

"But last night," Allen went on, "I had dinner with her son, Tommy, and learned something more about this lady. She told me that she didn't have any medical problems, and while that may be true, it's hard to see how her personal history doesn't influence what we do here.

"The McClanahans are from rural eastern Kentucky, up in the Appalachians. Her oldest son, Tommy's brother, was killed in a hunting accident a little over a year ago. He lost his footing on wet rocks while crossing a creek. He fell, struck his head, and drowned. Her husband was a logger, about the only work available in the area. Six months ago he was killed with another man when a tree fell on them. Mrs. McClanahan and Tommy have been going it alone ever since. Tommy was only fourteen at the time and couldn't do much work. His dad's old boss took pity on them and has been paying Tommy twenty dollars a day to run errands and fetch tools. This is what they have been living on. Tommy hasn't gone to school since his dad died.

"Remember those storms last week?" Allen asked, and then continued without waiting for a reply. "Well, they dumped more than ten inches of rain in one day over eastern Kentucky. Flash floods devastated the area. The trailer that the McClanahans lived in was trashed and they lost most of their possessions, although I think they had already sold most everything of value by that time. So there they were—homeless, feeling desperate, and living out of their twenty-five-year-old Chevy. The only family Mrs. McClanahan knew about was a brother-in-law working in Detroit. They used the last of their money to buy gasoline. They hoped it would be enough to get them to Detroit and a new life.

"The car made it this far before it died," Allen added. "We called the garage that towed it for the police. They told us that the towing fees were more than the car was worth. The tires are bald and there wasn't a drop of oil in it."

It's amazing how quiet a room can be, even one filled with people that just hours before had seemed irritatingly noisy. Even the coldness was gone. Every pair of eyes was fixed on Allen, many moist with emotion. "That's quite a story, Allen," I said, somewhat at a loss for words.

With elbows planted firmly on the table, Allen sat with his face resting in his hands. He looked embarrassed, an emotion that seemed strangely new to him. With a deep breath and another sigh he looked up and said, "Well, there's more.

"I was feeling very put upon when I was asked to take Tommy to dinner last night," he admitted. "I had a lot of work to do and I've been falling behind in my reading. I thought I was too busy. I thought the task was too menial. I thought I was too important. When I handed Tommy a tray, he just stood there in the middle of the cafeteria like a deer in headlights. I thought he was just shy, but then I realized that he didn't know what to do. He had never been in a cafeteria before.

"It was one shock after another last night, each more jolting than the one that came before. His eyes were as large as softballs as I told him where to go and what to do. When we got to the entrées, he stood paralyzed, almost frightened. He didn't know what to take because he didn't know what anything was. I was in disbelief as I struggled to explain stuffed peppers and chow mien. I didn't have a clue what to do with beef stroganoff. But it was watching him stand in front of the desserts that will haunt me for the rest of my life. He had tears in his eyes when I insisted that he take something. His hand shook when he reached for the chocolate cake. He knew what chocolate cake was, he had just never had any before."

Allen paused for several moments, as if stopping to rest while carrying a heavy load. His colleagues sat astonished, never before so touched during rounds. With another deep breath, and yet another sigh, he continued his story.

"I should have felt good watching Tommy eat, but I didn't. He literally inhaled his food. It wasn't until that moment that I knew he had been hungry, not the kind of hunger we have when we are late for lunch, but something more, something beyond our comprehension. It was hard for him to admit that they hadn't eaten that day, or the day before. They had spent all of their money on gasoline for the trip and thought that they could tough it out until they made it to Detroit.

"When they did eat, I don't think they ever had much. Their money could buy a lot of beans and rice, and Mrs. McClanahan baked bread. His dad and brother were good hunters and when they were alive the family usually had some sort of fresh game for dinner. Tommy didn't like hunting. He just couldn't bring himself to pull the trigger. Once or twice a week, however, he was usually able to pull a catfish out of the creek. But his mom had to clean them. Store-bought food was unheard of. Dessert was a special luxury—blackberries in the spring and pawpaws in the summer.

"When we were finished, I noticed that Tommy didn't eat his cake. When I asked him why, he told me that he wanted to take it to his mother. I protested, reminding him that he liked dessert and never had chocolate cake before. With a big grin he told me that his mother would be so surprised and that he was so grateful to have something to give her. It was all I that I could do to keep myself composed while I bought a second piece of cake. I've never seen a happier person than Tommy as he walked back to his mother's room with a piece of chocolate cake in each hand—one to eat and one to share. There was no doubt in my mind which piece he was going to enjoy more."

Allen reached out and picked up the box of bagels that had made its way around the table. "We take this for granted, but it's beyond the McClanahans' comprehension. I've never been hungry before—that's beyond my comprehension. Before last night, I've never considered the possibility that people I would ever meet might be hungry. I blew it big time last night. I couldn't see it when it was sitting right in front of me."

His distress was palpable and I felt a little guilty for not being more supportive the night before. There had been a change in Allen throughout his presentation. I was aware of it, but yet, I couldn't quite put my finger on what was different. His voice had grown softer, his choice of words less technical, the practiced assuredness a little less certain and more spontaneous. They were all subtle things in and of themselves, but taken together I found myself listening not to the judgment of the honor medical student, but to caring from the heart of a man.

"I've been up most of the night wondering how many others I have missed," Allen confided, his eyes now locked onto mine, as if searching for his answers within me, "afraid that I will never see the important things. How can I be a doctor without that? So, sir, I need to know how you knew that Tommy was hungry."

"I didn't know, Allen," I reassured him, "at least not to the degree that you discovered. I only knew that there was much more to their story than we knew about. But you know, all of the clues were there—their worn clothes, the way Mrs. McClanahan didn't want to eat, but seemed very preoccupied over her dinner tray, the way Tommy kept looking at her food.

"But Allen, I don't see your work yesterday as irrelevant at all. As a matter of fact, your workup, diagnosis, and treatment plan are right on the mark. Nothing you have told us today changes the fact that Mrs. McClanahan has a respiratory tract infection and is fatigued. You admitted her for observation, just in case something might have been brewing that wasn't obvious last night. In the light of day, your diagnosis remains correct.

"It would have been medically appropriate to have discharged her from the emergency room last night, just like you wanted to do, just like most physicians would have done. You have spent four years learning the right way to do things, learning how to do things by the book. Now you are in a position to put that knowledge to work, to take medicine out for a test spin. What has you so distressed now is the realization that practicing good medicine may not be enough.

"Some doctors go through their entire careers without learning that simple reality. They are good doctors, they do everything right, they follow every guideline, every study. But they could be more."

Rounds can be the definition of distraction. Pages, nurses providing patient updates, final touches to put on patient write-ups, orders to sign, and just plain fatigue all compete for the fragile attention of the post-call house staff. It's rare to have everyone's attention during rounds, something that drives young faculty crazy. Time has made me pragmatic about such things, and I no longer take it personally. I'm usually happy to have the attention of half my team at any given moment. But at that moment, every pair of eyes was trained on me, just as they had been with Allen, intrigued and captured by the drama that was unfolding before them. It was more than the medicine they had grown accustomed to, and perhaps been numbed by. It was something deeper than that. It was life itself.

"Some of us never see the person beneath the patient. We treat the shell for illness without ever cracking it and learning what lies beneath. We focus on medical history without considering, or maybe purposely avoiding, personal history. Social problems are nothing new in this hospital, and often it's difficult to avoid our patients' personal histories. They wear them like clothing and they're eager for you to know the source of all of their problems—a parent, a boss, the way they look.

"Personal history is simply a trail that we have left behind. If we stop and look back at the footprints we have left in the sand, they stop where we stop. The footprints do not travel ahead and pull us along. They do not tell us which path to take, or how fast we should walk. They are simply a remembrance that we have passed that way.

"As we stand in that sand and look back at our past, at those footprints, we do not move forward. We do not make new footprints. This is the problem with most of our patients, and maybe for most of us. We become victims of our past. It is possible for us to be victims only when we relinquish the responsibility for our lives to others, or to things we believe to be outside our control. If people or forces beyond our control are responsible for our problems, then we have to also look outside of ourselves for solutions to those problems. As we stand looking back at our footprints, waiting for the responsible forces that got us to that point to come to our rescue and create solutions for us, the sand before us remains smooth and unblemished, and we stop moving forward in our lives.

"It's only when we can take responsibility for the circumstances of our lives that we have the power to change them. Our past is important, but only as a journal of our journey, footprints to help mark our way as we move into tomorrow.

"We have all sat spellbound listening to Mrs. McClanahan's story. I think each of us would agree that her personal history, her past, is crucial to understanding not only her medical problems, but what needs she might have. If anyone has been victimized by their past, it's this family. But yet they don't act like victims. In fact, they never volunteered their past. Three or four docs spoke with this lady before her admission, myself included, and no one appreciated the immensity of her silence.

"The scarcity and challenge we have heard about this morning is heart wrenching and has brought most of us to tears. But I suspect this family would see it differently—abundance instead of scarcity, opportunity instead of challenge. It takes a lot of courage to leave everything that you know behind and travel to a new city to start a new life.

"What can we do to help the McClanahans, Allen?" I asked. "Should we get social service involved?"

Allen looked a little sheepish and said, "Well, I sort of already did. I hope it's all right. I asked for an emergency consultation last night. The social worker and I spent a couple of hours telephoning McClanahans. You may be interested to know that there are well over a hundred McClanahans in the Detroit area. Mrs. McClanahan thought that her brother-in-law's name was Albert. Turns out that Albert is his middle name. His first name is Zachary, which, of course, made him the last person on our list.

"He's actually a very nice man and wasn't aware that his brother had died. It was hard for them to keep in touch. Neither of them had vacation time and his brother didn't even have a telephone. He is going to meet his nephew and sister-in-law at the bus station tonight."

"How are they going to buy bus tickets?" I asked. "It doesn't sound like they have any money."

"We have that covered too," Allen reassured me. "The social worker suggested that I call some of the area churches to investigate any charities that might be able to help. I picked a couple churches out of the book at random and the first one I called was able to help. Actually it's quite a coincidence. A former pastor of theirs was treated at this hospital before he died from cancer. As a memorial to him, a fund was established to help people hospitalized here. They are going to buy the tickets and provide some money for food.

"We've all made calls home and have gathered up clothing and odds and ends for them to take with them. The hospital is going to pay for a cab to get them to the bus station this afternoon." Allen concluded.

I was very impressed, and said so. This medical student, who had appeared detached and distant from his patients only the day before, was now interwoven into the fabric of their lives.

"I hope all of this hard work is not rejected," I thought out loud. "They seem very proud."

"I was worried about that too," Allen replied, "and she looked like she was going to say no when I talked with her this morning. But I told her that it wasn't a gift. It was a just a step on a stairway of helping. I told her that others had helped me and the only way I can repay the favor is if someone lets me help them. I told her about the pastor and the congregation that thought so highly of him. As long as people accepted their help, his work and spirit would live on. I told her that the help was only a loan, that someday she would repay it by helping someone else, building that stairway ever higher.

"I don't think she wanted to accept the help, but she didn't want to hurt our feelings even more. So everything should be all set for them to leave the hospital today," Allen concluded.

With that, rounds came to an end. As was usually the case, the room cleared rapidly. The remainder of the residents' day would be a lost battle between time and patient needs. Allen was typically the first one out the door, clutching the clipboard that organized his day—but not this day. He remained behind, sitting motionless at the conference room table. He looked troubled, and a few years older than he had the day before. Alone in the room, I got up from my seat and moved next to him.

"Allen, that was outstanding work last night," I told him.

"Actually, I need to apologize for last night. I had to be dragged kicking and screaming to do the right thing. Ever since I was a child I wanted to be a doctor. I had this idealistic fantasy of helping people, being able to touch the lives of others and to know that I had made a difference. I realized in the wee hours of the morning that I had lost that dream somewhere on the path. Journal articles, board scores, and knowing the right answer had become more important than those people," he said with a hint of sadness in his voice.

"And how did you feel when you told us your arrangements for the McClanahans just a short while ago?" I asked.

Allen grinned at me. "Like I was a small boy again, dreaming about being a doctor. I'm excited."

"Never forget that feeling," I urged. "It's yours to experience every day. Sometimes, though, we forget to look for it. Like a beautiful painting hanging on a wall, it can eventually become routine and drab. The beauty is still there, it's just that no one looks at the picture anymore. You have nothing to apologize for, Allen. None of this would be happening for the McClanahans had it not been for you. I gave you a little nudge, but you took a simple act of kindness and made it sing. You did more than ask the right questions. You listened to the answers, and then you did what few are able or willing to do. You felt those answers and the spirit they came from. You made conscious contact with another soul.

"You have to marvel at the twists of fate here. If not for a run-of-the-mill viral infection, Mrs. McClanahan never would have been brought to the hospital. If not for a broken-down car, they might be lost in Detroit right now. If not for the severe storms, their journey never would have started. But I'm more fascinated with how their fate interacts with the fates of others, with your fate. What are the odds of their car breaking down in our city, of them being brought to our hospital, of your team being on call, of you being assigned their case, of having a hungry boy thrust on you, of you needing to feel the power of medicine?

"Most would call this coincidence, but you know, the longer I practice medicine the more I believe that there is no such thing. Things happen for a reason. We don't have to understand it, but if we can at least accept it as a possibility, we open our minds to infinite potential.

"Docs have powerful egos. We want to control everything in our lives and everything around us. Rather than considering the possibility of some outside force, everything we can't control we chalk up to chance. But it just doesn't work. The man who has a heart attack in the lobby of the hospital after visiting a sick friend, the woman who stumbles across the health fair at the mall and discovers that she's diabetic, the boy who visits his grandmother only to find that she has fallen and she's unable to get up—there's a pattern in the randomness. We are among the privileged few who are invited into the lives of others. We can taste fantasy, feel disappointments, revel in accomplishments, and even learn great secrets of life, if only we choose to linger for a moment and explore what our patients bring to us.

"What are the odds that a medical student, fatigued and perhaps a little disillusioned with the reality of medicine, finds the exhilaration and mission that he had always longed for in the lives of an Appalachian woman and her son? Last night was no accident. You will never forget these people. Every patient that you will ever care for will benefit from the lessons you learned last night.

"Just outstanding work, Allen," I complimented again, "and some pretty profound wisdom too. With what you told Mrs. McClanahan about the money and the opportunity to help others, you made it possible for her to accept your help."

"Well, it wasn't my wisdom," Allen admitted. "I have no idea where those words came from, I certainly didn't plan them or even think about them. They were just there."

As we sat for a few moments in silence, I found myself taking great pleasure in his smile. He still looked tired, but there was an unmistakable feeling of peace from him. He was going to be a special physician. As we stood up to leave, I stopped him.

"Wait a minute, Allen. You said the church fund was established in honor of a former pastor. Did they tell you his name?"

"I think it's on the check they dropped off," he replied, leafing through some papers on his clipboard. "Here it is. The Reverend Paul E. Prescot Memorial."

"Now why doesn't that surprise me," I said in a soft voice.

"Do you know this name?" he asked.

I smiled with the recollection of happy memories. It seemed so long ago, when in fact, it was only a moment ago in the changing fortunes of time. "Yes," I exhaled softly, "he was a patient of mine. But more important, he was one of my teachers, just as the McClanahans are yours. I was going to comment on what a coincidence it is for his name to pop up, but you know, there are no coincidences."

Hours later I was riding down the same elevator that I had ridden up in that morning. This time, I was its only occupant, but I was not alone. I was accompanied by the memory of Paul Prescot and his lessons of life. I felt strangely fulfilled. It had been a good day. Earlier, in that elevator, I had contemplated the wisdom of medicine. I had wondered how it could be taught, only to watch it happen a short time later. Paul had taught that class. Paul, with the help of his friends.

CHAPTER 10

Life Can Be Such a Headache

*Yesterday is but today's memory,
and tomorrow is today's dream.*
KAHLIL GIBRAN

*The quest for certainty blocks the search for meaning.
Uncertainty is the very condition to impel man
to unfold his powers.*
ERICH FROMM

Months when I acted as an attending physician always took me back in time. My memories of my own training years were always the most vivid during these days, the illusion of time more transparent. Hardly a day passed when an image or conversation wouldn't take me back to another time.

Time has an interesting effect on memories. It can soften, enhance, and even rewrite our recollections of reality. Like most, I look back on those early years fondly, sometimes with a longing to return to a simpler place in my life. It was a time when I would forge my closest friendships, encounter love, and first experience the power of impacting the lives of others. During these months, as I watched students navigate the hurdles that would initiate them into the profession and interns move from theory to practice, those memories became fresh enough to taste. Often, it was a bitter taste.

There was nothing fun about residency. It represented years of fatigue, frustration, and often sadness. It was the sadness that was most elusive in my memories, but I could often see it in the eyes of my young colleagues and remember its sting in my own heart. It was something that was never spoken of, an experience faculty would deny ever having, and a feeling that seemed somehow wrong to have. Medicine can be a sad business in those early days, and the sadness can grow into despair, or propel a life to new levels of understanding.

By and large, medical school and residency were merely an extension of adolescence, additional steps on the continuum that progressed through high school and college. While they were unquestionably adults, few students or residents had experienced working lives or commitments to anything greater than themselves. They led lives still sheltered from professional reality, and many would not drift far from their colleagues socially. Like adolescents, the cloth from which they had been cut had a thread of immortality running through it. Residency might be hard today, but there would be a tomorrow and it would be grand. It was a certainty.

Long, sleepless nights of call and days made heavy by decisions they seemed too young to make inevitably led to a reassessment of career choices during those training years. It was a terrifying thought. Had their years of investment brought them to something that they did not like, or could not do?

It was the structure of medical education itself, however, that fed the sadness of residency, or at least kept medicine's rewards well hidden. For the most part, medicine is practiced in offices and outpatient settings. Only a small percentage of patients ever require hospitalization, but it is the hospital where physicians learn their trade. Instead of seeing the hundred patients who get better, the one who doesn't becomes fixed in the consciousness of the student.

No matter how sheltered a life they led, nothing could protect the residents from colliding headlong with uncertainty. Little is certain in the hospital. It is a place where few patients want to be, and though predictions of good outcomes abound, it is also a place that reminds us that time is not ours to master. It unfolds according to the wisdom of the universe, independent of human intention and understanding. Tomorrow is but a thought, a picture that has yet to be painted. Medicine thrives on the certainty of tomorrow, but it is an illusion. These can be difficult lessons, lessons that touched my ward team particularly hard one week.

Tamra Watkins was a gifted intern. She knew the literature and how to make theory relevant to patient care. Her diagnostic skills were among the best that I had ever seen in a resident, and her management plans never sacrificed common sense. She was very good with people, and easily formed a bond with her patients and their families. It was a bond made possible by rare empathic skills. Not only could she sense her patients' feelings, but she experienced their thoughts, expectations, and fears vicariously. It was a gift that came with a price, however. The low, slow energies of fear and worry that swirled throughout the hospital clung to her like lint. She could walk to a bedside happy, only to leave sad and frightened.

Whereas Tamra knew the medical literature, Gretta Scott wrote it. She came to medicine as a productive researcher with a PhD in molecular chemistry, bringing her analytical skills to the patients' bedsides. Those expecting a rigid and serious physician, however, were invariably surprised by a personality rich with humor and happiness. She too, was good with people, but instead of absorbing the emotions of others, she left part of herself with them. Her mere presence could transform the sullen moods of patients and colleagues alike. Internship had thrust Tamra and Gretta together, and through its trials, they had become the best of friends. Their complementary gifts with people made them a dynamic team. I could see them as partners in practice together. But first, there were lessons to learn.

Morning rounds were dragging. The team was post-call—they had been working all night, and it had been a busy one. We had already discussed ten new admissions, and there was still more to do. Everyone looked exhausted. Even the medical students had been up all night, helping their residents gather laboratory data and complete paperwork. I was impressed with the way they had come together as a team, not so much to help each other out, although they clearly wanted to help one another, but to provide good care for their patients. Somewhere during the heat of battle, "your patient" and "my patient" became "our patients." It was a lesson that was never covered in medical school lectures or found in the pages of medical journals. It was a lesson that could only be learned through service to others, and I was very pleased.

The routine of emphysema, diabetes, alcoholic cirrhosis, and heart disease was broken when Tamra presented Brian Kirby. She had saved him for last. Perhaps she thought that his was the most interesting case she had received, but I suspected that she wanted to delay discussing him for as long as possible. It would inevitably make her feel bad again.

"Brian Kirby," Tamra told us, "is a twenty-one-year-old college senior without significant past medical history. He is not aware of any family health problems; he does not take medication, and has no allergies. He hasn't seen a doctor since his physical before starting college. He doesn't smoke, doesn't use drugs, but he does drink on the weekends with his friends. He is an honor student and plans to graduate at the end of this semester. He has been accepted at an Ivy League law school for the fall, and will spend the summer interning for a U.S. senator in Washington.

"This kid has it together," Tamra added. "My parents would adopt him in a second as the son they never had.

"Yesterday," she continued, "Brian and three of his friends were getting ready to head to Florida for spring break. Spirits were high and nobody detected anything out of the ordinary, other than Brian going on the trip. His friends told me that it took a lot of coaxing to get him to go—he had intended to stay behind and study. They hadn't been on the road more than twenty minutes when Brian slumped to the floor of their van and started to have convulsions. They turned around and came here.

"The convulsions lasted for about a minute and involved all of his extremities in rhythmic flexion and extension with arching of his back. He was incontinent of urine. After the convulsions stopped, he appeared to be in a deep sleep, with slow, deep respiration. In the emergency room he had another episode, described by the charge nurse as a tonic clonic seizure. It resolved with an IV of lorazapam. Chest X-ray and EKG were normal and with the exception of a mild metabolic acidosis, all of his laboratory studies were normal as well."

Not once during her presentation did Tamra look down at her notes, adding to the air of confidence that always seemed to be with her. "What's your impression, Dr. Watkins?" I asked.

"Brian is a healthy young adult with a normal clinical exam who was admitted for new onset seizure," she summarized. "The metabolic acidosis was probably from the seizure activity, and it has resolved on labs this morning. The differential diagnosis of new onset seizure is epilepsy, infection, toxic or metabolic etiologies, and a CNS lesion. His exam and labs do not support infection or metabolic causes. Although he denied drug use, I did blood and urine toxicology screens and both came back clean."

"That leaves this," Tamra said, picking up a large red folder from the table. The sadness in her voice was not predictive of good news in that envelope. "We were able to get an emergency head CT done this morning, and he just came back from it."

I was shocked when Tamra placed the CT films on the light box. Even sitting fifteen feet away, I could clearly see trouble. I could feel it too—that same sickening sensation in the pit of the stomach you feel watching a horrible accident, powerless to stop it. Most of the normal brain tissue in the frontal lobes had been replaced by tumor.

Tamra pointed out the abnormal features on the scan for the team. "The tumor is huge," she said. "It measures twelve centimeters across at its greatest point. I figure it's a meningioma or a glioblastoma, and judging by the extension across the midline, I suspect that it's malignant, not that that is going to matter much. Even if it's benign, to remove this surgically would probably be neurologically devastating."

"It's amazing that he hasn't had any symptoms before now," Gretta interjected. "This thing has been there for months. A biopsy is going to be important to be able to make a tissue diagnosis. If it is malignant, then the median survival is only about a year. And that's after surgery, radiation, and chemotherapy."

"It hardly seems worth it," Tamra argued. "To subject this boy to a brain biopsy and horrendous treatments just to give him a year—it seems wrong."

"If it's benign, he could have three years or more," Gretta tried to reassure her friend.

Tamra didn't look reassured. "I know we're supposed to be ecstatic with numbers like that, but when you're twenty-one, the difference between one year and three doesn't seem all that great. But you know, your comment about his symptoms touches a nerve. This is one of the sickest patients I have ever had, but he is also the healthiest-looking patient that I have ever had. He looks like he could run a marathon. Two days ago, he was the picture of health. Today we are talking about his mortality. Nothing has really changed. The tumor was there before, and just as large. The only difference now is the shadows and shapes on a CT. He was feeling great this morning when I saw him. All of that is about to change."

While those gifted with compassion and empathy tend to make special physicians, it comes at a price. It is difficult to tell someone bad news, but these physicians agonize more than most. They hurt twice, first in the delivery of the message, and then through sharing their patient's fear, anger, and despair. And so it was with Tamra when she shared the news with her patient, and forever changed his concept of time. She also shared herself, as few physicians can. She was a sister, a friend, and when it was helpful, a concerned stranger. It was a process that was difficult to watch. I wanted so much to be able to tell her that it got easier with time, but for physicians like Tamra, it never would.

To the distress of Tamra, and the disbelief of Gretta, Brian Kirby left the hospital the following day to continue spring break with his friends. It wasn't a treatment option in any of the journal articles that they had read. Tamra felt that the hospital could provide greater comfort and safety. Gretta was certain that the hospital would prolong survival. They were to learn a lesson in patient autonomy. People have a right to make their own decisions, even bad decisions.

Prior to his departure, I stood in the corner of his room quietly listening as his doctors attempted to change his mind. Brian readily admitted that he hadn't been very interested in going to Florida initially, but it suddenly became the most important thing in his life. He had planned on studying over spring break, not for the joy of studying, but for the rewards it would bring later. The friends who were to accompany him seldom left his bedside during that hospital stay, and most of the time they just sat together in silence. It wasn't until those periods of silence that Brian ever looked at his friends, and felt their presence. He had been programmed to always prepare for the next step: college, law school, and politics. He didn't know much about now, but that was where his friends could be found, and that was where he wanted to spend the next week. With reluctance, his doctors agreed to prescribe medication to prevent additional seizures and to delay further evaluation until his return. They didn't understand what he was trying to tell them about experiencing now, only the logic that one more week would not change anything.

The lessons of ward months can be difficult ones to learn, but they seldom linger long in the thoughts, pushed aside, at least for a short time, by new patients with new problems. Such was the case with Brian. As he was leaving the hospital, Steve Market and Joyce Bonner were in the emergency room.

I was early for rounds the following morning, but Gretta and Tamra were already in the conference room, each sipping from a mug of hot chocolate. They looked tired, as all residents do post-call. Their smiles seemed different that morning, more out of habit than expressions that sprung from the inner being.

"Tough night?" I asked, as the rest of the team filed into the conference room.

"Nothing that chocolate can't handle," Gretta commented wryly.

"I don't know," Tamra retorted. "This is my third cup and I don't feel any better."

While Tamra and Gretta immersed themselves deeply into chocolate therapy, the medical students each presented a patient they had admitted. The pharmacy student discussed the use of diuretics in the management of hypertension. The social worker reviewed the indications for nursing-home placement. Finally, we learned what had driven the interns to chocolate.

Dr. Scott flipped an X-ray on the conference room light box and sat on the corner of the table to discuss her patient. It was a chest X-ray, showing an enlarged heart and haziness throughout both lungs that looked like pulmonary edema. "Steve Market is a twenty-seven-year-old man without," she started.

"Excuse me, Gretta," I interrupted. "How old did you say he is?"

She gave me a knowing glance and repeated, "He's twenty-seven."

I kept silent, not wanting to interfere with her presentation, knowing already that the story we were about to hear would be disturbing.

"Mr. Market," Gretta continued, "is a schoolteacher. He teaches high school science. He hasn't had any medical problems, although there have been some concerns about infertility after four years of trying to have children. It isn't a concern anymore, as his wife is six months pregnant with twins. He keeps a picture of the ultrasound in his pocket and shows everyone who walks into his room.

"Mr. Market was in his usual state of health until three or four weeks ago, when he had several days of congestion, cough, and myalgias. His symptoms did not seem severe enough to warrant a trip to the doctor, and gradually resolved. Since that time, however, he has felt tired and has been easy to fatigue. His exercise tolerance has progressively declined over the past several weeks. He used to run five miles every day without fail. Fatigue and shortness of breath have forced him to stop at progressively shorter distances. The past few days he has felt winded just by walking. It was when he awoke early this morning gasping for air that his wife brought him to the emergency room.

"Physical examination revealed a well-nourished and well-developed man. His blood pressure was low, heart rate elevated, and his oxygen saturation was only 88 percent. This improved to 100 percent on two liters of nasal oxygen and he felt much better. He had distended neck veins, crackles throughout the entire lung fields, and edema of the lower extremities. All of the routine laboratory studies were normal. As can be seen on his chest X-ray, he has pulmonary edema.

"Clinically," Gretta summarized, "this is a classic picture of congestive heart failure. My grandfather has CHF, and his chest X-ray looks better than this one. The real question is, why does a twenty-seven-year-old have it?"

"What have you done for him?" I asked.

"We started him on diuretics and got a dramatic response. He's put out four liters of urine in the past twelve hours. This morning, his shortness of breath is gone and he has been walking the halls without the fatigue that he had been experiencing. To confirm the diagnosis, we had an emergency echocardiogram done late yesterday. The cardiologist who looked at it estimated the left ventricular ejection fraction at 10 percent."

It was a number that brought gasps throughout the room. Even the medical students appeared shocked. Ejection fraction is a measure of how well the heart squeezes. A healthy heart, certainly that of a twenty-seven-year-old, would be expected to have an ejection fraction near 70 percent. Clearly this was not a healthy heart.

"I suspect the diagnosis will be idiopathic cardiomyopathy," Gretta said, "most likely from that viral illness he had a few weeks back. We will need a biopsy to confirm it, but one thing is evident now. This man's life has changed forever. Considering the severity of his heart failure, he may very well require a heart transplant."

"Isn't it amazing," Tamra observed, "what a run-of-the-mill virus can do. Most of us get some aches and a cough. One of millions will get a destroyed heart. I've been sitting here wondering—why him? What made his heart a good target? And why now? They worked so hard to have a family. Two days ago his future was painting a nursery. Now it's a question of survival. How quickly life can change."

"I think that was the theme yesterday, that life can quickly change," Tamra solemnly said, getting up to place her own X-rays on the light box. Expecting pathology, I looked closely at the chest X-ray, but it looked normal to me. Whatever it was that we were going to hear about, the films provided no clues.

"Joyce Bonner is a thirty-two-year-old lady, employed as a fitness trainer at a local health club." Tamra started. "She is healthy, but she does take medication for high cholesterol. Her husband picked her up from work and they were on their way home with pizza and rented movies. It was family night and their two children were waiting for them.

"They were stopped, waiting for a red light. It had been raining for a short time, but the intensity of the wind and rain escalated suddenly and very dramatically. As the rain was falling sideways, Joyce called home to check on the kids and to remind them to close the windows. Her call ended abruptly with a thunderous crash and the sound of breaking glass and crushing metal.

"Although she had never been in an accident before, she knew that they must have been hit by another car. She knew little else. It happened so fast that she didn't see anything coming. She didn't even hear the screeching of brakes. Joyce felt very disoriented. It had been a well-lighted intersection, but everything was now dark. She could feel the dash; it was covered with broken glass but the air bags had not deployed. Something cold and wet kept brushing back and forth across her face.

"Joyce's calls out to her husband were returned by silence. She reached out to him, but something large and rough obstructed her effort. Reaching under the object she was able to feel his arm, and followed it down to his hand. She squeezed that hand and was intensely thankful that it squeezed back. They sat together in silence, in strange darkness, and amid strange sensations. But there was nothing strange about that hand, and she waited in the comfort of its grasp."

Tamra paused for a moment, took a sip of her chocolate, and continued her tale. "After what seemed like an eternity to Joyce, sirens and the sound of trucks broke the quiet. The darkness was pieced by intense light, but through its glare she was unable to see anything. A concerned voice spoke to her. It was a paramedic. Rescue was not far away, but first they had to be cut from the wreckage. A coat was placed over her face to protect her as the sounds of power saws sprang to life.

"As she waited with her husband for freedom, she was struck by the strangeness of the sounds around her. She had expected the cutting of metal to sound different. She could almost imagine standing in the woods and watching lumberjacks at work. Strange too was the hand that she clung to. It had turned cold, but she felt a closeness that went beyond what they had experienced even through intimacy.

"Eventually, the cutting stopped and many hands lifted her from the car and onto a stretcher. As she was wheeled away, Joyce looked back to the shock that had been waiting for her. The car was nearly flattened, a huge tree lying across it. She was amazed that they had lived through it.

"In the emergency room, Joyce learned that, in fact, both of them hadn't lived through it. Her husband had died, his chest impaled by a large branch. Miraculously, she was uninjured. Examination, laboratory work, and X-rays were all unremarkable. She was admitted because of some chest pain she had in the ER. Most likely the pain was musculoskeletal," Tamra concluded.

"My God," Gretta exclaimed. "One minute you are thinking about eating pizza and watching a movie and the next minute you are a widow with two children to care for. How is she dealing with this?"

"She is sad, but is doing much better than I would have expected," Tamra replied. "I would be hysterical. I think being responsible for the kids is helping her. They stayed with a neighbor last night and will be brought to the hospital later this morning. She will tell them about their dad then. I also wonder how much denial she has. She keeps talking about how close she was with him last night, forming a bond that will never weaken. He was either dead or dying when they were in the car together."

"Why do we always call it denial when someone doesn't react to adversity the way we think that they should?" Gretta asked. "I'm pretty narrow-minded when it comes to challenging logic and convention, but you know, why couldn't Joyce's experience have been from conscious contact with another spirit? It is no more incredible than having a tree fall on you in the middle of a city intersection. Some would call that an act of God. Why couldn't both be?"

It was a question that seemed strangely out of place in our world of science and medicine, and while it was a question that Gretta did not expect an answer to, it was one that was hard to dismiss from our thoughts. It was a question that would slip into my awareness repeatedly throughout the remainder of the day, and as I sat in my darkened study before retiring that night, I realized that the answer was not important. Asking the question, however, was. If we never ask the question, we will never seek the answer. If we never seek the answer, it will never be found.

The team would not have long to consider those metaphysical and epistemological aspects of medicine. New revelations were waiting along the path that we were all walking together. As Joyce Bonner was spending her first day as a single parent at home, Carol Waterfum was playing volleyball.

Carol was a twenty-four-year-old graduate student at the local university. She was working on her MBA, but she allowed herself the diversion of sand volleyball. It was one of her passions, and she felt she had too few passions. There would be time for passion after she had made it to the executive boardroom. For volleyball, however, she would participate competitively two afternoons each week. It wasn't all a waste of time, she rationalized. Keeping her aggressive skills finely tuned would serve her well in the business world.

Carol played hard that day. She always played hard. While serving during the last set, she experienced sudden and intense head pain. The serve sailed over the line, something that never happened to her. She completed the set without her teammates noticing anything was wrong. Her boyfriend knew, however. He attended all of her games and knew from her play that something was amiss. They had been sweethearts since junior high school and had attended the same college together. As he drove her home, he tried to recall an earlier time when she had mentioned a headache. He couldn't.

Throughout the day, Carol's headache worsened. Her boyfriend went to the drugstore for her, but none of the over-the-counter pain relievers helped her discomfort. Against her wishes, he spent the night on her couch. He was afraid to leave her. The light hurt her eyes and even the ticking of the clock was uncomfortable for her. When she awoke in the early morning hours screaming in pain, he bundled her up, placed her in his car, and drove to the emergency department of the teaching hospital.

Carol's boyfriend felt sick with worry during the drive to the hospital. He had never seen her ill before, or even considered it a possibility. That only happened to others. The two made for a good couple. Everyone thought so. His friends and family often chided him for not marrying her, but if the truth be known, he had tried numerous times. Carol had plans; a family would make it difficult to achieve the success she wanted from life. There was plenty of time to settle down later.

In the emergency room, Carol's headache continued and worsened, if that was possible. It had spread from the back of her head to the top. Her eyes hurt and she heard a constant tone in her ears. Even her hair hurt. It wasn't until the fourth injection of morphine that the pain seemed better, and Carol was able to fall off to sleep.

Carol worried the doctor in the emergency room. She had used the magic words in describing her pain, words that even medical students recognized as ominous. "This is the worst headache of my life." As would be expected of a young, healthy woman, her laboratory studies were entirely normal. With the exception of her left pupil being larger than the right, the physical examination was also normal, but that single exception was alarming. She was admitted to the medical service and assigned to Gretta's care.

Normally I would not have learned about Carol until the following morning on rounds, but Gretta asked me to look in while she met her new patient. Gretta was concerned that Carol would need surgery and didn't want her to be whisked away to the surgical service before I had a chance to see her.

"Ms. Waterfum?" Gretta asked as she approached the young lady's bedside. "I'm Dr. Scott and I'm going to be taking care of you. How is the pain?"

A grim face looked back at her. "That's some dope you have here. I still have a headache, but I just don't give a damn," her patient responded. "Please, call me Carol. Mrs. Waterfum is my mother."

"Your boyfriend told the emergency room doctor that your father died from a stroke when you were young," Gretta said. "Could you tell me more about that?"

Carol had a faraway look in her eyes, but I couldn't tell if it was because of the medication or if she was searching distant memories. "I was pretty young and I don't remember him much. Mom told me that he died from a brain hemorrhage. He was thirty-two. His brother died of the same thing at the age of thirty. I believe that their dad died of a stroke or something when he was in his twenties. Why do you want to know about—" Carol started to ask before falling silent in midsentence.

"Oh my God!" Carol exclaimed, her face showing a mixture of shock and fear. "Is that what I have?"

Gretta sat on the side of Carol's bed and reached for her hand. "I don't know what the problem is yet, Carol," Gretta replied in the softest, most reassuring voice I had ever heard. "Some problems are genetic and can be inherited. That's why we ask about family history. I am a little concerned that there may be a problem in your brain. Your pupils are a little unequal and the CT scan of your head suggests that there may be a problem in some of the blood vessels there. We won't know for sure until we can get a better look with a high-tech scanner."

Carol looked anything but reassured, and Gretta, still holding her hand, continued. "We are going to be partners in this, Carol. I will tell you everything that is being done and the results of all the tests. I'm not going to hide anything, and I'm not going to lie to you.

"Look, Carol," Gretta explained. "There is nothing in this world that can be as frightening or as terrible as that which we can imagine. Concentrate on all of the good things in your life, like maybe your boyfriend, who hasn't left the waiting room since you arrived, and I'll work on getting answers for you."

A tear rolled from the corner of Carol's left eye as she looked up at Gretta and smiled. "It's a deal."

Standing in the nursing station on Carol's floor, I complimented Gretta on her bedside manner. She put her patient to ease with honesty and caring. In fact, she even had me feeling more at peace by the time we were done. Gretta had scheduled an MRA, an angiogram using a powerful magnet rather than X-rays to make the images of Carol's brain. If Gretta's hunch was right, we would need the neurosurgeons later that evening.

When I walked into the conference room the following morning for rounds, a group of medical students was huddled around the light box. Gretta was teaching, explaining techniques and anatomical structures. She made a good teacher. Peering over their shoulders, I could tell it was an MRA of the brain.

"Is this Carol's?" I asked.

Gretta nodded in affirmation. "It's what we thought it would be," she said. "It's a berry aneurysm."

It seemed an understatement standing there looking at the films. I had never seen one as large, even in textbooks. There were actually three of them, the largest upwards of two centimeters in diameter. No wonder she had a headache. It was amazing she hadn't had one long ago.

"Does she know?" I asked.

"Yes, sir," Gretta responded. "I told her last night because I wanted the neurosurgeons to see her right away. I didn't want her to learn about it from them. I can't do anything to help her, but I can at least be there for her."

"Don't underestimate the power of your presence," I said softly. "What did the neurosurgeons say?"

"They don't have much to offer her. The location and size of the largest aneurysm makes it unresectable, and to try to operate on the smaller ones would likely cause the big one to rupture. They talked about putting a catheter in and embolizing them, but the lesion is just too large. The bad news, as if having them isn't bad enough, is that the large aneurysm has started to leak, which explains the headache. She has obviously had these for some time without symptoms. The increased blood pressure during the volleyball game probably caused the hemorrhaging. Fortunately it was only a small amount and it stopped quickly, but it could rupture at any time."

After rounds, Gretta and I went together to see Carol. It was a trip that neither of us was looking forward to. "I'm dreading this," she told me. "Does it ever get easier, telling people bad news?"

I had to think about it for a moment before answering. "No, it's never easy, but you get to a point where you understand what people's needs are and you can sometimes make it easier for them. When you stop and think about it, information is neither bad nor good—it's how our minds process that information that makes it bad news or good news. Most of us have no trouble looking someone in the eye and showing them comfort when we give them news that we believe they will find good. Feeling and extending that same closeness when the news will be judged bad can be a powerful tool in medicine.

"Look, Gretta," I insisted. "You did it last night. You told Carol about her aneurysm so that she wouldn't hear it from the surgeons. That certainly wasn't for the surgeons' benefit. Your telling Carol didn't change the facts any, but I'm certain it changed the way she saw those facts. Instead of a being a messenger, you were a participant. When you reach out and touch a life, you actually become, if only for the briefest of moments, a part of that life. In that moment you can make a difference."

Carol was sitting up in bed when we walked into her room, her boyfriend sitting on its side. They were holding hands. Her appearance wasn't what I had expected. She was smiling and looked happy.

"Dr. Scott," Carol gleamed. "We were just talking about you. I don't think you have met Troy, my boyfriend."

Introductions were exchanged, and Gretta asked, "How are you feeling, Carol?"

"I feel great," Carol said. "The headache is gone. It wasn't until it resolved that I realized how much we take feeling good for granted. Not having the headache is only part of it though. You are a large part of it. It is difficult to explain, but the time you spent with me last night made me look at myself in a way I had never done before. It felt like somebody holding an umbrella for me in a rainstorm. When I looked in that mirror, I liked who I saw."

"I'm glad the headache is gone, Carol." Gretta said with obvious relief in her voice. "The neurosurgeons don't think you need to stay in the hospital, but they do want you to think about going to the specialty center in Baltimore as soon as possible. They might have something to offer that we don't."

Carol smiled even more broadly and said, "Thanks, but maybe later. First, Troy and I are getting married—tomorrow. Then we are going to travel. We don't know where, or for how long."

"Do you think that's wise?" Gretta asked with a look of concern.

"I wouldn't have before last night," Carol explained patiently, "but right now, absolutely. Look, I know this thing that I have is terminal. It is going to blow and I don't know when. Chuckles the surgeon would have me believe that it's going to be sooner rather than later. I was freaked out by that thought, but, you know, life is terminal. There is no certainty of a tomorrow. I've certainly been living like there is, however.

"When you always have tomorrow, it's too easy to waste today. I've spent so much time looking ahead that I couldn't see happiness right in front of me. And here he sits. If I drop dead on the altar tomorrow, I will have known moments of happiness that might otherwise have slipped by my life unknown. Thank you so much for helping me see that."

When Gretta and I left Carol's room, Tamra was waiting and walked us the short distance to the staff lounge. Three large steaming cups sat on the table.

"I thought the two of you could use some chocolate." Tamra said with a knowing smile. "How did it go?" she asked her friend.

"I don't have the slightest idea." Gretta sighed as we all sat down together. "I'm not even sure I know what happened in there. I think that she just thanked me for telling her the worst news of her life. I should be feeling horrible right now, but part of me feels good—at least the part of me that's not numb."

Looking thoughtful, Tamra said softly, "I wish I was numb. The beating has been relentless this week. I actually ache. Just when I think I've seen the saddest thing that life can whip up, there is a new surprise standing behind door number two. I'm starting to get paranoid, half expecting a meteor to fall on me."

Gretta smiled at her friend. "Perhaps you should sit on the other side of the table," she joked. "I know what you mean about feeling down. You expect to encounter bad things in medicine, but it has just hit too close to home this week. They are all our age. It could have happened to any one of us. "

"Gretta, you said that part of you felt good about Carol." I said. "Why?"

"I could only see darkness in her situation," Gretta said, "but she found some light—an opportunity to examine her life and find meaning. That I might have helped her discovery, even without meaning to, makes me feel good."

"I keep thinking about Brian Kirby." Tamra noted. "He's probably sitting on a beach right now, and I bet there's a friend nearby. I couldn't think of anything more important for him to be doing right now than radiation treatment. He discovered a greater importance. I'm a little embarrassed about that."

"No need for embarrassment, Tamra," I noted. "You just wanted the best for him, and doctors are taught that the best is measured in milligrams of drugs and millirads of radiation. I can't help but believe that there is a part of each of us that always knows what is best, that always knows what is right. We all feel intuition or hear that little voice from within, but few of us have the courage to get out of its way and follow it.

"Look," I asked, "what were the moods of Brian and Carol like after their life-altering news sunk in?"

"Brian was happy when he left the hospital," Tamra noted, "actually excited at spending time with people who he didn't seem that close to before."

"As far as Carol goes," Gretta observed, "she's positively glowing. You would swear she's been waiting years for the day she gets married."

"There is a theory," I suggested, "that one's mood reflects the correctness of one's actions. Happy people are on the paths that are good for them, finding peace and experiencing meaning. Sad people are not. I see it all the time in the office, and if I trust that observation I find it easier to help people."

"That's a Native American concept," Tamra said. "When you are close to your spirit it can be seen in your face and felt in your eyes."

"It's the same in most Eastern philosophies," Gretta noted.

"I suspect that it appears in most spiritual systems," I agreed. "The point is that in the midst of seeming tragedy, Carol and Brian both found something of value. We can all share in that piece of happiness."

I paused to take another sip of chocolate. It was quite good. Maybe Tamra and Gretta had something here; an antidote for those things that make it difficult to hear our inner voices.

"It has been an unusual week, indeed. There was Brian and Carol, Steve Market, and of course Joyce Bonner. Did you notice anything similar about their stories?"

We sat in silence drinking our hot chocolate. It was a good two or three minutes before Gretta put her cup down, smiled, and turned to me. "Uncertainty," she said. "Each illustrates the power of uncertainty."

"Yes," I said. "Life can change in the blink of an eye. Uncertainty is just something that we must come to terms with, both in our physical lives, and spiritually. It can be a curse, or for those who understand its mystery, a powerful tool. For those who seek meaning in distant goals and future times, uncertainty can steal their dreams. But for those who embrace uncertainty, life exists in the present moment, and their dreams can be lived."

Tamra and Gretta would encounter uncertainty many more times that month, just as I had throughout my career. It wraps around our patients' lives and participates in every plan and every dream. It is like water on pavement; it finds every crack and crevice. While the idea was disturbing at first, Tamra and Gretta would eventually come to see it as a gift. What is evident when looking at the lives of others can be difficult to see when looking in the mirror. Carol Waterfum and Brian Kirby would be their teachers, reminding them that uncertainty touched their own lives, and that it offered them an opportunity to unfold the power of their lives as well.

CHAPTER 11

You Can Take It with You

*Every man goes down to his death bearing in his hands
only that which he has given away.*
PERSIAN PROVERB

*I don't know what your destiny will be, but one thing I do
know: the only ones among you who will be really happy are
those who have sought and found how to serve.*
ALBERT SCHWEITZER

Early in my career I was astonished at the number of
unhappy people I encountered. Those were days of learning while I practiced in the outpatient clinic of the teaching
hospital. Many of my patients were poor, and I attributed
their unhappiness to scarcity and the social challenges that
poverty brought. But private practice would eventually take
me to the affluence of suburbia and the startling realization
that people there were not any happier. In fact, some of my
happiest patients came from meager means.

Unhappiness comes packaged in many ways: depression, fatigue, chronic pain, or a host of other maladies that spawn in the darkness of the low energy that many sustain and nurture. It is a part of every office day, an encounter that is not without risk. The energy of one person's unhappiness can reach out and envelop those nearby, leaving them feeling exhausted and sad.

It is no wonder that so many of our residents dislike going to the clinic. For decades medical educators have searched for reasons. Work hours have been shortened, support staff has been supplemented, and lunch has even been provided, but many residents still dislike the experience. The impact of the energy in which the physician is immersed goes unrecognized.

Among the most confusing and difficult problems that the physician encounters are people who are happy in their unhappiness. They come to the office with symptoms and fears of a horrible disease. Detailed histories and thorough examinations fail to uncover significant problems, launching extensive laboratory and diagnostic studies. The good news of a clean bill of health, however, is met with disbelief and anger. Convinced that something awful was missed, these patients often seek a new physician.

Occasionally patients will come to the office with the insight that they are unhappy. They seek no studies, no medicine, and no magic. The simplicity of their plea touches deeply: how can they find happiness? Their quest seems as elusive as it is simple, and certainly most physicians would agree that it is beyond the scope of medicine—but not beyond the scope of healing. If unhappiness is an infirmity of low energy, then perhaps its cure is one of energy as well.

If the medical clinic was my first exposure as a physician to the illness of unhappiness, it seems only fitting that that was where I would start to find its remedy.

The medical clinic was a daunting place for an intern. But it was a place where I very much wanted to be. Unlike most of my colleagues, I had an inkling that I wanted to practice primary care medicine, so I had a vested interest in learning as much as I could about outpatient medicine. Still, it was hard to consider it an enjoyable experience. We were always locked in a battle with time, and we were always losing.

There is no such thing as a routine problem when you are an intern in medical clinic. Even as you are starting to get the hang of hospital medicine, you are a fish out of water in the outpatient setting, the arena that will someday become your world. A simple blood pressure check would take twice the amount of time allotted for that patient. A simple rash would drive us to the textbooks while the clock ticked away. Such simple problems, however, were cause for celebration. Most of our patients had extensive problems and numerous medications. Writing prescriptions seemed to be our life's work. Running behind schedule, and the stress that came with it, became a way of life.

If the challenges of clinic were not enough, our time there was haunted by the feeling that there was some other place that we should be. Medical education was a creature of tradition, and tradition dictated that medicine was learned on the hospital wards, not in the clinic. Thoughts of our patients in the hospital and the work that remained to be done there accompanied us to every examination room and every patient encounter.

The intern's greatest test came on post-call days in clinic. Fatigue accompanied the intern, who had last slept a day and a half earlier, to each patient visit. As we struggled to make it through the day, the patients became our enemy.

It was not hard to find unhappiness in clinic. Its energy hung in the air, sapping the strength from all who entered. Patients, doctors, and staff, no one wanted to be there. But it was a wonderful place to learn not only medicine, but ourselves. It was a wonderful way to explore life's energy, what could diminish it and what could cause it to soar to unknown heights. It was on this expedition that Ryan Charles would help me find my way.

I met Ryan Charles the evening before we started internship together. A welcoming party at the home of our department chairman had thrust the intern class together for the first time. It was not a relaxed gathering. Our preoccupation with the day to come hardly made for a festive atmosphere. Ryan seemed to stand out among us. He seemed happy, and if he was anxious, he hid it exceptionally well. It is my first recollection of being in the presence of someone, a perfect stranger, and feeling uplifted and at peace. Judging by the crowd that always surrounded him, that feeling was shared by others. Without knowing a thing about him, we had little doubt that he would become one of our leaders.

Ryan's schedule was remarkably similar to my own. We rotated through the same hospitals together, had ward service on the same months, and even spent the same afternoon in medical clinic. The coincidence that had placed us together elated me, and it would lead to a close friendship. But now I know that there are no coincidences. Our meeting and the friendship that has spanned decades was meant to happen. I had things to learn.

I can't remember Ryan ever complaining during residency. He was always happy, and more often than not, he made the rest of us happy. During the holidays, his uniform always included a red Santa hat with white fur trim. He wore it everywhere. I recall arriving late for grand rounds one day. The weekly conference was the most important educational function of the department, and it attracted experts from the community and the medical center. Standing in the back of the room, I looked out over the filled auditorium for an empty seat. In the midst of a sea of white-coated, white-haired men sat Ryan wearing his Santa hat.

As you would expect, Ryan was a hit with the patients. He considered it a personal challenge to coax a smile from the most cantankerous and obnoxious of patients. Invariably he was successful, and it did not go unnoticed by the rest of us that his patients always seemed to get better quicker than ours did.

Ryan fascinated me in clinic. Like the rest of us, he frequently arrived looking exhausted. By the end of the day, however, he seemed refreshed and strangely happy. I often accused him of napping on his exam room table as the rest of us saw patients.

If his hospitalized patients liked him, then his clinic patients adored him. He was always in demand and his schedule was frequently overbooked with people who wanted to see him and only him. At the end of each visit, Ryan could be seen escorting his patients to the waiting room with his arm wrapped around them. They were invariably happy. A happy patient in medical clinic was even harder to find than a happy doctor. Many commented that they felt better just by talking to Dr. Charles.

It was on a busy afternoon in the clinic that my understanding of this happiness germinated, ironically from a seed planted in the poor soil of unhappiness and irrigated with low energy from negative human emotions. Ryan and I were both assigned to ward services at the teaching hospital. It had been an unusually busy stretch, and even Ryan looked fatigued, a reliable barometer of difficult times. Finishing my patient list early, I sought him out to see if he needed any help. He was post-call and most likely running on empty. From nurses to unit clerks, everyone looked out for the post-call resident.

In Ryan's examination room sat an older lady with a kind face and an easy smile. She clutched a cane and had a diagnosis written all over her: arthritis. Ryan, however, was nowhere to be found. It didn't take long to discover him in an empty exam room. He was sitting at the desk with a half dozen pill bottles and a prescription pad spread out before him. I was about to speak when I saw him do something curious. He removed a twenty-dollar bill from his shirt pocket, folded it into a compact square, and placed it inside the cap of one of the pill bottles.

"Ryan, what are you doing?" I asked

He jumped in surprise and exclaimed, "Nothing! Oh, hi. Where do you bury your dead? You scared me half to death."

His face went from startled surprise to a flushed red, much like that of a child whose hand was just caught in a cookie jar. "I was just refilling meds," he said.

I smiled broadly at his discomfort. Clearly he was rattled, unsure just how much I had seen. "I'd offer to help, but I don't think I put as much into my refills as you do," I teased.

Ryan leaned back into his chair and sighed deeply in resignation. "Okay," he said. "I just need a couple of minutes to finish up with Mrs. Smith and then I'm done. Can we talk then?"

"Sure thing," I said. I'll wait for you."

"Uh, you won't . . ." he said, then trailed off.

"I won't say a word, Ryan," I assured him. Grinning like a kid, he gathered up his papers and pill bottles and disappeared down the hall.

It was not long until I heard Ryan's voice as he escorted Mrs. Smith down the long hall of the clinic to the waiting room. She walked with a slow, measured gait, uncomfortably slow for those of us always in a hurry. But Ryan kept pace with her, step by step, his hand resting on her back. To those who didn't know them, she could have been his grandmother. As they approached, I heard her say, "Remember, Dr. Charles, we are expecting you at our ice cream social."

Ryan and I left the clinic together. We walked for a couple of minutes in silence along the labyrinth of tunnels beneath the medical center when he stopped and rested against the cement wall.

"She's poor, Bill," he said. "It's not a lot of money, unless you don't have any. She thinks that she has a guardian angel in the pharmacy. She is so thankful to have some money in her purse."

"That's one of the most unselfish things I've ever heard of, Ryan," I said. "Do you do this a lot?"

"Just with a few patients," he mumbled, clearly embarrassed.

"Are you going to the ice cream social?" I asked, half-joking.

"Sure," he replied. "It's such a small thing and will make such a big difference to her. I've even gone to one of my patients' home for dinner."

"You're kidding me!" I said, clearly surprised. "Is that a safe thing to do around this neighborhood?"

"Perhaps not," he admitted, "but it was all she had to give. She hadn't had visitors for years and she was so proud of her home. It was a huge deal for her and did more good than a hundred office visits."

"You seem embarrassed by this, Ryan," I said. "I'm overwhelmed by your generosity. You put the rest of us to shame."

Ryan was thoughtful for a few moments, and then replied, "I think maybe I am embarrassed, but not for reasons that you think. It's not altruism. It should be, but it's not. I do it because it makes me feel good. There is a powerful energy in giving and helping. I feel the most incredible peace and happiness after I've been able to give something away. Clinic is a great place for that. We can get so close to people there. All we have to do is take the opportunity. It might be good for them, but it's even better for us. If I leave clinic upset, it's because I didn't take the opportunity to give.

"Look at all of our colleagues," he continued. "Everyone is postponing happiness until they finish residency or fellowship. We've bought the nonsense that we have to pay our dues by being miserable before the rewards come without question. It doesn't have to be. We can have it now." Ryan paused, looked up at the ceiling, and smiled broadly. "You know, Mrs. Smith just made me realize that as good as helping can feel, giving someone else the opportunity to help can be even better.

"She was telling me about the money that she found last month. She spent some of it on fresh fruit, something she gave up long ago as an extravagance. Every day she would go to the park and enjoy an apple or a pear. She savored those moments when simplicity made life exquisite. She had half of the money left, which she was saving for hard times. Knowing that she had it made her feel safe, and she liked the feeling. At church one Sunday she learned about a young mother with three children who had breast cancer. A collection was being taken to help the family. She gave her money.

"Mrs. Smith told me that as much as she liked having fruit and the security of some money in her purse, nothing gave her more joy than being able to help someone. She told me that she goes to bed each night with that warm feeling and gratitude for having been able to give."

The story of Mrs. Smith and the passion with which Ryan told it touched me deeply. I was very proud of my friend and grateful for the reminder that opportunities to help others surround us constantly.

"That's a wonderful story," I said. "Isn't it amazing how many people were touched by one simple act of kindness?"

"It's truly energy," Ryan said thoughtfully. "It flows from one person to another. I didn't set out to do anything special. I just wanted to help her out a bit. I'm not even sure it was an act of kindness, because I knew it would make me feel good. To see how one simple act can touch so many people awes me, though.

"Usually we don't get to see the effects of kindness, and that's the way it should be. We give simply to give, because it makes us feel good. Otherwise, our ego starts looking for credit. But if you stop to think about it, the giving of something doesn't end with the recipient. The energy is passed on to someone else, and as long as no one breaks the chain, it can flow forever."

"By breaking the chain, you mean not giving to someone else?" I asked.

"No," Ryan said, "by not receiving. Only when a circuit is complete can energy flow. I can have the best of intentions and a great capacity to help, but I cannot give if there is not somebody also willing to receive."

"That's what you meant about your patient who invited you to her home for dinner, that it was all she had to give," I suggested.

"Yes," Ryan said, smiling. "I never thought much about it until then, but it was the happiest that I had ever seen that lady, and I suspect it was the happiest she had been in many years. That lady taught me a lot about myself, and from that day I have tried very hard never to say no."

Internship is synonymous with learning, and the slope of the learning curve is quite steep. When I look back to those years, perhaps the most important lessons I learned were the ones Ryan shared with me. The seeds he planted that year found fertile soil. I have little doubt that most people enter medicine with the desire to serve, and my colleagues were typical of that. That we had something to give, however, even in those early days, was a bit of a revelation. The most we had to give was also what we had the least of: time. That reality made the gift of time all the more precious. Most of us gave that time: time to listen to a patient's story, time to explain to the confused, and even time simply to be present. It made us feel good.

There is a part of each of us that has the desire to serve. It is the conduit for the flow of energy in the universe. Most of us, however, have forgotten what seems instinctive in child-hood, how to give of ourselves. In others, the conduits have become too corroded for energy to pass. Perhaps it's due to all of those lectures, but physicians tend to have the dirtiest wiring. Many want to help, they just don't know how.

Those early predictions of Ryan's ability were accurate. He became a leader in the residency program as well as in the community. While still a resident, he founded Medical Volunteers, an organization that paired nurses, doctors, and other health professionals with the needs of the community. Teams were dispatched to local homeless shelters, senior centers, housing complexes, anywhere there were people in need. Ryan understood energy well. By bringing together those who wanted to give with those in need willing to receive, the circuit was completed and energy flowed. That energy is still flowing today.

Helping others doesn't require an organization. Nor does it require the skills learned in medical school and the habits acquired in residency. It is an ability that we have carried with us from our childhood, and like the rules of hide-and-seek, have long forgotten. Physicians have vast resources to call upon in the service of others: the finest of medications, cutting-edge technology, and access to the latest research. True generosity flows from the simplest of our assets, however: the capacity to listen and the willingness to share our lives.

If my patients have been my greatest teachers of medicine, the residents and students I have watched through the years have best shown the power of giving. Medical residents spend three years serving, but it does not seem like serving to them. Their value to others is difficult for them to see. Their acts of service are buried among too many patients, too many tasks, too little time, and too little sleep. They feel far from being doctors, and often far from being caring people. But a special place offers them the opportunity, not only to give of themselves, but to appreciate the impact that giving has upon others.

An hour's drive from my home there is a place of great beauty, with rolling hills, hardwood forests, crystal-clear streams, and of course, birds. Trips to those hills brought peace to a calm ravaged by schedules, responsibility, and the expectations of others. The beauty of the area could not hide the poverty and scarcity that is life in Appalachia, however. Need lived along dirt roads in every hollow and every clearing. It was the stimulus that led to the creation of a free clinic at the county health department.

I first approached health department officials about starting a free clinic thirteen years ago. It was only politeness to outsiders that tempered initial opposition and created a willingness to at least consider accepting the services of volunteer physicians. I was surprised by their skepticism and suspicion. While they acknowledged the community's immense need, disappointment was as common as poverty in the area, and broken promises would only make their needs hurt more.

As I waited for a meeting with county leaders to discuss the clinic proposal, I couldn't help but notice the aging photographs that adorned the walls of the meeting room. History was preserved there: steam thrashers at work, county fairs, barn raisings, and neighbor helping neighbor. The pictures reminded me of photographs of the early teaching hospital that hung on the walls of the medical clinic, turning my thoughts to Ryan and the lessons of those days. There truly was energy in the desire to serve, but willingness was not enough. Before that energy could flow, it needed someone to receive it.

Despite the county's reservations, skepticism, and history of disappointment, the plans for the clinic were approved. With the circuit complete, the energy started to flow that day and has never slowed. While the clinic was founded based on need, the energy that drove the clinic and made it special was the same as the energy in the beauty of the hills, the forests, the crystal-clear streams, and the souls who make it their home.

Few things have brought more meaning into my professional and personal life than the health department clinic. At first I was uncertain who benefited more from the clinic. I no longer doubt it; I receive much more than I give there. It has made manifest the idealistic fantasy of healing that once lived only in my childhood thoughts. In recent years, residents from the teaching hospital have made the Friday afternoon journey to the health department clinic. I didn't think the rewards could grow greater, but they proved me wrong.

In the health department clinic the residents would find little of what they had grown accustomed to at the teaching hospital. Supplies were limited and laboratory studies and diagnostics were often nonexistent. What they did find, however, was an abundance of patients in need, and themselves. In themselves, they found powerful tools for healing: touch, listening, and a caring heart. We all found great lessons in life.

As special as I found my work in clinic, the exchange between the residents and their patients was nothing less than magical. Special moments in clinic were the rule rather than the exception, but one experience in particular will never be far from my thoughts.

Tom was just a few weeks into his internship when he encountered Mr. Johnson at the health department clinic. Like many of our patients, Mr. Johnson had emphysema, but it seemed unusually severe for his forty years. He had no money and no way to buy medications. Tom had seen Mr. Johnson two weeks earlier and sent him home with an inhaler. Samples were scarce, but Tom found more to bring with him on his return trip. They would keep his patient in medication for several months. The weather had been unusually hot, and Tom was worried when he learned that his patient didn't have air conditioning. In one short visit, Tom had grown attached to and somewhat protective of this man who cut firewood for a living.

For someone who had seen Mr. Johnson just two weeks earlier, Tom was spending a lot of time with him in the exam room. It was early in the clinic session and we were already falling behind. When they finally emerged from the room, Mr. Johnson's eyes were red and moist. It was obvious he had been crying, something quite unexpected from the gruff outdoorsman.

"Mr. Johnson," I asked, "what's wrong?"

There was disbelief in his eyes and also a pleading for help. "Dr. Tom bought me an air conditioner," he said. "Nobody's ever done anything like that for me before. I can't get it home, though. Can we work things out later?"

I assured Mr. Johnson that I understood and he made a hasty and awkward exit from the clinic. When the last of our patients had left for the day, Tom and I sat down to talk over Cokes.

"That was pretty nice what you did for Mr. Johnson," I said.

"It was supposed to be just between the two of us," he said, clearly embarrassed. "I was worried about him and I wanted to help. It feels really good, even though I botched it. I didn't think about how he was going to get it home.

"It's a good model," he said, growing increasingly excited. "It shouldn't be very expensive to operate. I could use a hand getting it out of the car. Where would be the best place to put it for Mr. Johnson to pick up?"

I took a deep breath and sighed. "Tom," I said softly, "about the air conditioner. You either need to take it back or give it to someone else. Maybe we can think of something else for Mr. Johnson."

"Why?" he asked, his voice cracking. "Did I do something wrong?"

"No, Tom," I reassured, "and I'm very proud of you. But Mr. Johnson lives in a small camper up in the hills. He has no running water, he bathes in a creek that runs nearby, he heats and cooks with wood, and he has no electricity. He has no place to plug in an air conditioner."

A look of shocked horror spread across Tom's face. "My God," he said, "what have I done? Instead of helping, I just called attention to everything that he doesn't have. Why didn't he tell me?"

"He didn't want to hurt your feelings," I replied. "You wanted to give him a precious gift, and you did. Didn't you see his face? The gift wasn't the air conditioner. The gift was you. The gift was your caring."

To this day, the health department clinic is a special place. It is a place where the commodity of energy is given and taken. It is a place were patients leave with hearts filled with appreciation, feeling good that someone cares. It is a place where residents leave feeling purposeful and inspired, perhaps for the first time in their careers. It is an energy that they will always recognize, and will always know how to use.

Medicine brings boundless opportunity to those who struggle to learn its secrets and practice its art. Perhaps the greatest is the opportunity to give. The greatness is in its simplicity and ubiquity. There is hardly a moment that passes that we do not have something that we can give to others: a smile, cheerfulness on the telephone, or even a door held open. The most important tool of medicine is time to listen— a realization that has taken me a career to learn, or rather, a career of patients to teach. Time is also our greatest gift.

In medicine there are days when it is difficult to find peace in our work, as I'm certain there are in all professions. The cynical among us would ask if this is not the nature of the work. If giving makes us feel good, then perhaps the converse might be true as well; not feeling good is a reflection of not giving. It's something that Ryan tried to explain to me many years ago. Maybe unhappiness is merely a spiritual message to remind us that we can be of service.

The more I learn about the nature of people, particularly that part not discussed in medical texts, the easier it becomes to serve. Sometimes the need is so overwhelming, with patient after patient expressing unhappiness, that I find myself slipping into the comforting numbness of textbook medicine. No doubt this is a healthy defense strategy to separate us from the pain of our patients, but it also limits the potential for healing. I am learning to avoid that feeling of numbness. When I find my equanimity challenged, I silently ask, how may I serve?

Patricia Morduck would test that ability. A sixty-two-year-old college professor, mother of three, and grandmother of twelve, she was eating Mother's Day dinner at a local restaurant with a sizeable number of family members. It was a good day for Mrs. Morduck, who always found it difficult to gather the large family together. It was during dessert that she developed a mild headache, her speech became garbled, the left side of her face drooped, and she fell unconscious to the floor.

The doctors in the emergency room diagnosed a hemorrhagic stroke. She had a long and complicated hospitalization, including surgery to evacuate the blood in the brain After the stoke extended to adjacent brain tissue, she required more surgery. After a month in the hospital she spent another six weeks at a rehabilitation center.

Mrs. Morduck came to my office the day after her release from rehabilitation. Even with the walker, it was obvious she had significant weakness on her right side. Her gait was painfully slow, and it took her a full minute to go the short distance from exam room door to chair. There was still some drooping on the left side of her face, and her speech was thick and pressured, with the consistency of cold syrup.

When I sat down to talk with her, it quickly became apparent that obtaining her history would be difficult. She met each question with long periods of thought, as if searching for the right words, followed by syllables and phrases that sounded like a foreign tongue. Each time she realized that she was not being understood, she repeated the process, only with greater volume.

In frustration, I turned to her husband for help in obtaining the needed information. Mrs. Morduck flew into a rage, slapping her left hand against the table.

"No, no, no," she screamed. "Me talk, me talk."

Her husband, clearly embarrassed, held up his hands in surrender. "I'm sorry, doctor," he said. "She's been like this all through rehab. She won't accept help doing things or let people speak for her."

My frustration forced an obvious glance at my watch, something that I taught my students never to do. Fifteen minutes had passed and I hadn't learned anything that would be useful in caring for this difficult patient. Excusing myself under the pretense that I needed to answer a page, I retreated to the security of the file room. I stood with closed eyes leaning against a wall trying to collect my thoughts. The waiting room was full, I was already behind schedule, and it was going to get much worse. I was more than frustrated, I actually felt angry. But my anger was not at my schedule or out of vague circumstance; it was directed at that lady sitting in my room who couldn't even say her name. It was a disturbing awareness, one that brought me no peace.

One question seemed to rise from the darkness where I found myself. How may I serve? Stranger still was the prompt answer, one that seemed so obvious that a child would know it. Take the time to listen.

I asked my staff to apologize to the patients who were waiting, advise them that I would be at least an hour behind, and offer to reschedule those who couldn't wait. I returned to Mrs. Morduck, apologized for the interruption, and placed my hand on hers.

"Mrs. Morduck," I said, "now tell me what you want me to know."

And tell me she did. Much of what she said I could not understand, but I knew it was not important whether or not I understood; only that I listened. While the examination required only five minutes that first visit, we spent nearly an hour talking. The anger and frustration that I had seen in her eyes slowly melted away, as did the anger and frustration that had intruded upon my peace.

It was not hard to understand her frustration. She was a college professor one day, struggling to communicate the next. The answers to her frustration would not come from medication, however. They would come with time and hard work, nurtured by the physical, speech, and occupational therapists. They would also come from the expectation of getting better and the knowledge that she was not her speech, her walk, or the comfort of those around her.

I felt strangely good when she left. I was hopelessly behind schedule and I had inconvenienced many people, but it seemed much less important than it had just one hour earlier. I had cured nothing, but I felt that I had helped. I couldn't help but wonder, though, if it would make a difference.

A month would pass before Mrs. Murdock's second visit with me. She was working hard but discouraged with her progress and the fatigue that accompanied her therapy. I applauded her accomplishments, however, noting that she had graduated from a walker to a cane and that her speech was much easier to understand.

She came without her husband on the third visit, walking without the cane. Surprisingly, she said very little, but when she did speak it was difficult to detect that she had ever had a stroke. Her eyes were uncommonly bright, and there was a peace about her that I hadn't felt before. I watched her feet when she stood to leave. Her gait was still somewhat tenuous. When those feet stopped at my chair I looked up at her. Stooping slightly, she kissed me gently on the cheek and quietly left the room.

I no longer question whether or not patients benefit from my efforts, appreciate them, or even understand them; it is irrelevant. We serve because that is what we do. It's how we express our true selves. It's how we find happiness.

CHAPTER 12

The Miracle of Healing

Do not pray for easy lives. Pray to be stronger men.
Do not pray for tasks equal to your powers. Pray for powers
equal to your tasks. Then the doing of your work shall be
no miracle, but you shall be the miracle.
PHILLIP BROOKS

There are only two ways to live your life.
One is as though nothing is a miracle.
The other is as though everything is a miracle.
ALBERT EINSTEIN

Doctors don't believe much in miracles. There are exceptions, of course, and I have come to recognize that they are often the best among us. For the most part, though, doctors are threatened by the concept of miracles, their egos balking at the possibility that something greater than themselves could heal others.

Some egos are so threatened by the prospect that their hosts are downright hostile to the suggestion of a miracle. For them, nothing happens that cannot be explained by the rational mind. The only reality is that which can be observed and explained through the principles of science.

Young physicians seem to struggle with this the most. Products of long apprenticeships based around the principle that cure comes through medicine and manipulation, they often feel threatened by the possibility of another kind of healing. Those in academic medicine toil to find their truths in logic and clinical research. It is the young academic physician who often wages the most pitched battles with the specter of miracles.

Such was the case with Ben Marsh, a young physician who joined the faculty of the teaching hospital right out of residency. He was cast from the mold of tradition, successfully indoctrinated by role models who clung to medicine's past. He had a kind heart, but he was rigid in his beliefs and expectations of others. He found his truths in the pages of the medical literature and patterned his practice upon them. It provided his ego the security, and the self-satisfaction, of knowing that everything he did was right.

Ben was obsessed with quality and passionate to instill his obsession in others. The more others became like him, the closer they could come to perfection. It was a crusade that frustrated his residents and brought his students to despair. There was no detail of their work too small to escape his scrutiny and intervention. The organization of their days, the order in which patients were examined on rounds, even the layout of their chart notes, all could be better if only they did it like him.

If it was unusual for residents to resist conforming to the will of their attending, it was unheard of for medical students to question a superior's wisdom. It would be a momentous event, and it occurred early one morning in a medical unit nursing station at the teaching hospital. I had just seen a patient of mine who had been admitted during the night, and I sat reviewing the chart and sipping a cup of coffee. Ben whisked into the room with his medical team streaming in behind him. His white coat was crisply starched and pressed and buttoned from top to bottom. His name was embroidered in red above the left pocket and a gold pen was clipped inside.

"We need to talk about what happened in there," Ben announced in a voice certain to be heard by all in the room. "It was totally unacceptable."

His team gathered around him, most looking uncomfortable under the gaze of the bystanders, who sensed that a spectacle was about to unfold. I was curious about Ben's choice of location for a discussion that was obviously going to be quite personal. A conference room that could have afforded privacy was just down the hall. I couldn't help but wonder if he wanted an audience.

"I can't believe that you told Mrs. Sutton that," Ben confronted one of the medical students standing before him. "Here we have a lady with metastatic cancer whose only hope is chemotherapy. She tells you that she wants to pray on it for a couple of days, and you tell her that it sounds like a good idea.

"When you wear that white coat," Ben went on, his hands gesticulating wildly, "you have no business imposing your religious beliefs on others or giving support to irrational decisions. We practice medicine here. We don't wait for miracles. Her answers will come from me, not prayer."

It was an assault that would have antagonized the most seasoned of residents and caused most medical students to lose all composure. But the object of Ben's wrath maintained quiet poise. He was an older student; in fact, he looked a good five to ten years older than Ben. He was a big man and stood a head taller than Ben. His face supported a full beard, which gave him an air of wisdom. Even under such duress, his face had a kind look, as if it would probably smile easily.

"Dr. Marsh," the student replied, "I would never impose my beliefs on someone else, be they a patient or not. At the same time, I would never show disrespect to someone's beliefs by suggesting that they were wrong. Prayer has nothing to do with religion. Don't underestimate the power of it, sir."

Ben stood in shocked silence. He had a confrontational style, one that served him well by stifling debate even among his colleagues. He achieved his victories with the surrender of his opponent. He was unaccustomed to discussions that continued beyond the point at which he dismissed them. Ben did not like being challenged; to have a challenge come from a medical student must have been a mortal wound. Ben would have been best served by moving on, but the ego seldom serves its host well.

"Doctor," Ben said with an edge of sarcasm in his voice, "we are men of science. We can offer only that which we can prove. Chemotherapy is efficacious for pancreatic cancer. Studies show it. Prayer is not science. People can't think their problems away."

"But Dr. Marsh," his student replied, "what about the placebo effect? We are taught that 30 percent of the action of every medication has nothing to do with its biochemical properties, but with the expectations of the person taking it. Don't those people get better by a mere thought? When we watch someone squeeze a lemon and our mouths water, is that not a mere thought that launched biological change in our bodies? Why is it so hard for us to accept the healing energy of thought just because we can't see it? We can't see sound, but we accept its presence."

"It's hard to accept because you can't prove it," Ben argued. "I can show you studies proving the value of chemotherapy. You can't do that with prayer. That's the problem that religions have and they hide behind it. Faith is the act of believing in something without any evidence to support it. You can never disprove it. The end result is that that poor lady has been given false hope."

"I couldn't disagree more, sir," his student responded. "The literature is full of examples of the positive impact faith and religion have on health. Patients who believe in a God fare better than nonbelievers when undergoing major surgery. Those who attend regular worship services live significantly longer than those who do not, and they tend to rate the quality of their lives higher. Our antidepressant medications work by increasing serotonin levels. Meditation has been shown to increase levels of serotonin, not only in the person who meditates, but even in those nearby and unaware of the meditation."

"That's crazy," scoffed Ben. "I've never seen such studies, and if they exist, they certainly couldn't stand up to rigorous scientific methods."

"Well, Dr. Marsh," the student replied, "we only find what we look for, and I suspect that many physicians would never look for such answers. I think your premise is shared by much of the medical profession, though, and that is unfortunate. We can prove chemotherapy works, but we can't disprove the power of faith? Why would anyone want to disprove faith? We don't have to be threatened by faith. Maybe we should find a way to combine the power of faith with that of medicine. Maybe that's where the cure for cancer will be found."

The medical student never raised his voice, never lost the calmness that seemed to define him. He had a quiet voice and the room had grown silent as everyone strained to hear his words.

"Prayer does indeed stand up to rigorous science," he continued. "Byrd published a prospective, randomized, double-blind study about the effect of intercessory prayer. For a year they followed patients admitted to a coronary care unit. Half the group, unbeknownst to them, was prayed for by individuals who believed in the power of prayer. The other half of the patients were not. Both groups received the same standard of care and their physicians did not know to which group the patients belonged. The prayer group fared significantly better during their hospitalizations, suffering fewer complications and having a less severe course of illness. Similar studies were published by Harris in Kansas City and Sicher in California.

"We tend to think of faith and science as incompatible, but I think that's just because our science has been too primitive to allow us to rationally deal with that which we cannot see. It has only been with the recent advent of quantum physics that we are starting to discover the science of spirituality. Einstein's theory of relativity and chaos theory are but a couple of examples. Everything is energy and there is some force out there that organizes it all.

"We can scoff at the possibility that thought is simply energy with limitless potential. Quantum physics brought us Heisenberg's Uncertainty Principle, which essentially tells us the observer changes that which is observed. We can't fathom the power of our thoughts. Can there be any coincidence that the people who have understood quantum physics the best, Albert Einstein and Max Planck to name just two, have been deeply spiritual beings? The idea that thoughts can create reality is not just a principle of quantum physics, it is a spiritual principle as well.

"Dr. Marsh," his student continued, "I don't think that any of us know enough to be skeptical about the power of prayer. Prayer, meditation, finding silence; these are all ways that people tap into the energy that connects them to the universe. Being open to such possibilities doesn't minimize what medicine can do, it makes the potential endless.

"With all due respect, sir, it's not prayer that gave our patient a false sense of hope. You told her that there was an 80 percent response rate to the chemotherapy. I believe that to be true, but that's not what she heard. We use terms like remission and response rates so inappropriately, almost like used car salesmen. Yes, there may be an 80 percent chance that her tumor will get smaller, her blood chemistry will improve, or any other parameter that we want to choose will give what we define as a response, but that's not what she heard. She heard cure. When all is said and done, with chemotherapy she has an 80 percent chance of being dead in one year, as opposed to within three months without it. And much of that year may be spent ill. I have no problems with it if that lady wants to reach down into the silence of her spirit and try to pull up a miracle."

"When you have more experience, doctor," Ben said dryly, "I think you will find that there are no such things as miracles."

"Actually, sir," his student replied with the hint of a smile, "I am hoping that with more experience you will be able to find them."

I had never seen Ben at a loss for words, or uncomfortable as the center of attention. I had no doubt that he regretted not having his discussion in private. To the surprise of his team, he dismissed rounds early and quickly left the floor. The smiles were ear to ear on every member of the team, except for the medical student who had stood his ground. For the first time since the conflict started, he appeared uncomfortable and set about to make himself as inconspicuous as possible at a computer terminal.

Curiosity got the best of me, and I quietly sat down next to the team leader.

"Who's the guy in the beard?" I asked quietly.

The resident smiled. "Oh, that's Thomas. He's a Jesuit with a doctorate in divinity. He was sent to medical school to become a doctor for some of their missions. He's a neat guy. A third-year medical student and I've never seen him flustered. It's going to be a great month."

I would see Thomas in passing every now and then at the teaching hospital, but we were never to meet or to have the talk that I would liked to have had. Still, he had impressed me and I found wisdom in his words that excited me greatly. Imagine, a scientific basis to spirituality that we were only starting to comprehend. Science was usually the weapon of skeptics and those seeking to disprove that something greater than ourselves exists. There is a wonderful irony in the possibility that our science has only recently evolved sufficiently for us to consider the most basic of the mysteries of the universe. I had never heard it described that way. Science was usually used only as criticism.

Thomas was right; I didn't know enough to be skeptical about such things. The idea that prayer and meditation could touch the energy that connects us with the universe was a startling concept to me, but not an entirely unfamiliar one. I had heard it before, or at least felt its presence among the myriad of patients who had come into my life. Those special patients, the ones who had touched me most deeply, had a special energy about them. I was starting to understand just what that energy was.

Thomas was right about miracles, too. They are everywhere in medicine, but often obscured in subtlety or lost among minds unable to marvel. With enough experience, though, even the most cynical in our profession witness healing that just shouldn't have happened, accomplish tasks beyond their skill, or find answers outside their knowledge. Thomas would call these miracles, and he would be right. They had visited my practice many times.

Eddie Que was a thirty-six-year old man without a health care in the world. He worked as a lineman for the electrical company, but that's not who he was. He was the man who enjoyed jazz Saturday nights and going to church Sunday mornings. He was the Little League coach and the number one fan of the football team. He was the person anyone with a problem came to to find unconditional help.

Most days at work, Eddie had lunch with his coworkers. He was a fun person to be around and made work seem less like work. One day, somewhere between his ham sandwich and his potato chips, Eddie experienced intense indigestion, profuse sweating, and slumped to the floor unconscious. His coworkers stared at his motionless form for a half minute or more, fully expecting him to get up and announce that it was all a joke. They had all learned CPR, and had all complained bitterly about the classes that their employer made them take. Had they known that they would be called upon to use it, they would have paid closer attention in class.

Eddie's best friend knelt by his body and checked for a pulse. It had been easier on the training mannequin; everyone knew that there wouldn't be a pulse. There wasn't one in

Eddie either, and he wasn't breathing. They called for help and Eddie's coworkers practiced the impossible. When the paramedics arrived, Eddie was still unconscious. A tube was placed into his airway so that the paramedics could breathe for him with a bag resuscitator. Electrodes placed to his chest connected him to the portable monitor, its screen revealing only random electrical activity, not the pattern of blips associated with a healthy heart. The paramedics knew it as ventricular fibrillation. Eddie's friend knew something terrible had happened. The paramedics started an IV and medicated him. They shocked him multiple times, but his cardiac rhythm remained stubbornly unchanged. Eddie would surely die if a rhythm of life could not be restored.

The paramedics were still doing CPR when the ambulance reached the emergency room at the teaching hospital. Blood was sent to the laboratory, Eddie was connected to a ventilator, and the doctors and nurses set about to bring rhythm back to his chaotic heart. Round after round of drugs was infused into his bloodstream, separated by attempts to electrically shock the heart into compliance. With each round the attempts grew more frantic. Forty minutes had passed by the time the cardiac monitor revealed a normal heart rhythm, more than an hour after he had fallen ill at work. Eddie remained unconscious and unresponsive. The brain cannot survive long without oxygen. The only thing that offered hope for his survival was that CPR had been started so promptly.

While the emergency room doctors were working on Eddie, a team of cardiologists and technicians had gathered in the cardiac catheterization laboratory. As soon as a normal heart pattern was restored, Eddie was wheeled into the laboratory. It was a procedure the cardiologists had done countless times, a routine that could almost instill boredom if it hadn't involved the human heart. The femoral artery was pierced at the groin and a catheter journeyed through the iliac artery and then the aorta before reaching the heart. The catheter was manipulated into the coronary arteries where contrast was injected to reveal the blood vessel on X-ray imaging. The problem was both obvious and dramatic.

The LAD, the left anterior descending coronary artery, the artery that sustains the majority of the pumping chamber of the heart, was totally blocked. They call it the widow-maker lesion, for good reason. Eddie had had a heart attack, and it was a major one.

The first catheter was replaced with a special one, one with a minute balloon at its tip. Within the blocked artery, the balloon was repeatedly expanded and relaxed until the blockage opened. Yet another catheter was introduced, this one with a stent, a small coiled spring, at its tip. The stent was placed where the blockage had been to keep the artery from closing again. The process was repeated on two other less severe blockages. It was the cutting edge of technology; the best medical science had to offer. Such capabilities had been unheard of just a few years earlier. Many would consider it miraculous.

From the cardiac catheterization laboratory, Eddie was taken to the coronary care unit. He remained unconscious, unresponsive, and on the ventilator. From a cardiac standpoint, he had done well, surviving what most people certainly would not have. But his doctors were concerned that he was not waking up, fearful that there had been brain damage caused by a lack of oxygen. With his condition unchanged on the second day, the neurologists were consulted.

Eddie's pupils were fixed and dilated. He did not respond to painful stimulation. When the ventilator was briefly turned off, he made no effort to breathe on his own. It was a constellation that had a tragic significance. Eddie was brain-dead.

The neurologists confirmed their diagnosis with an EEG and suggested that his wife consider organ donation.

The miracle was not that Eddie's friends were at his side when he needed help and that they knew what to do, although that was miraculous. The miracle was not that the emergency room team was able to restart a stopped heart, although that was also miraculous. The miracle was not the technology that can open an occluded coronary artery and restore life to a damaged heart, although it was miraculous as well. The miracle was not that through organ donation, life can continue even after death, although that too is miraculous. The miracle was that I saw Eddie in my office two weeks afterward, and continue to see him on a regular basis a decade later.

The day after Eddie was determined to be brain-dead with no hope for recovery, he woke up. It's one of those impossibilities that happen with uncomfortable frequency in medicine. The realization, or even the awareness of the possibility, that something greater than ourselves is at work in the universe stabs at our egos. I still see that neurologist at times at the teaching hospital. After all these years, it is difficult for him to accept that his premise, and not his technology, was wrong. His science just hasn't evolved sufficiently to explain, or even understand, the miracles that are woven into the fabric of medicine.

Once you start recognizing miracles, even if only to argue their rational explanations, you start to see them everywhere. It's much like buying a new car. Once you pull it off the lot you see the same model on every street. Medicine provides a special place from which to observe the miraculous manifested from the energy of life. Healing is more than observing, however; it is participating in the miraculous. I have been most deeply touched by those miracles that have disguised themselves as my skill, masqueraded as my knowledge, or hidden as my wisdom.

I had been in practice for only a few years when I received a call from a nurse who had shared office space with me at the teaching hospital. Her father was ill and she asked for my help. It was a call that would launch one of my greatest challenges, and plunge me deep into the world of miracles.

Sol Williams was sixty-eight, described by his family as cantankerous, proficient at golf, and exceptional at bridge. That would be a side of him that I would not see for many months. Every winter, he and his wife spent a month or two in Alabama. His last trip began no differently than the earlier ones, and the two settled into their usual routine of golf, dining out, and playing cards with friends. It would be while dining out that his routine would change.

During a meal of crab at their favorite restaurant, Sol became weak, nauseated, and light-headed. The fact that he did not argue about going to the hospital worried his wife the most, however. He avoided doctors scrupulously. In the emergency room, his blood pressure was found to be low, but otherwise his evaluation showed no abnormalities. With a tentative diagnosis of gastroenteritis, Sol was admitted to the hospital for observation. His blood pressure continued to fall, however, and within a day he had lapsed into a coma.

After three days of intense investigation, his doctors and specialists could not identify the cause of his illness, or seem to make headway in treating him. His family was frantic with worry. I was flattered by his daughter's call, but at the same time quite apprehensive. Her faith that I would know what to do for her father seemed obviously misplaced. With much reservation, I agreed to accept Sol in transfer and he was flown home by an air ambulance. At the very least, he would be closer to his family.

I met Sol and his wife for the first time in the intensive care unit. A kind, soft-spoken woman, Sol's wife would seldom leave his side in the days and weeks to come. Sol was unresponsive, his blood pressure supported by medication, and he was being fed by a tube passed through his nose to his stomach. I lost no time in getting our best specialists to his bedside. Neurologists, pulmonologists, cardiologists, and infectious disease doctors all weighed in on the origin of his mysterious illness, and naturally, each thought the answer lay within their own specialties.

Other than the trivial detail that Sol wouldn't wake up, his laboratory and diagnostic studies reflected the picture of health. His white blood cell count was slightly elevated and there was evidence of inflammation within his systems, so infection became our leading suspect. We cultured his sputum, blood, urine, stool, even his cerebrospinal fluid, but we could not locate a site of infection. I would have cultured his pillowcase if I thought it would have helped.

When science can't guide you, you guess. We did a lot of guessing with Sol, trying one antibiotic regimen after another, each more complicated that the one that came before it. If Sol's problem was infectious, we did not have the cure for it.

The cardiologists suggested a cardiovascular source of Sol's illness. They analyzed his blood for cardiac enzymes, obtained electrocardiograms, and performed echocardiograms. An ultrasound was done on the arteries of his neck. They even took him to the cardiac catheterization lab for an angiogram of the coronary arteries. There was no cardiovascular diagnosis to be found.

The neurologists reveled in the challenge. Perhaps Sol had suffered a stroke. When a CT of his head did not reveal one, Sol was taken to the brand-new MRI scanner. While the technology was exciting to employ, it did not provide any answers. Perhaps Sol's coma was due to seizure activity. His head was wired to the electroencephalogram, but days of recording failed to show a seizure. Unconvinced, the neurologists used trials of anticonvulsant medications. But Sol remained unconscious.

In desperation, a toxicologist was brought in. Perhaps there had been a toxin in the crabmeat that Sol had eaten. Blood, urine, stool, and even hair samples were sent to specialty laboratories around the world. No toxins could be identified.

With each new specialist and hypothesis, the Williams family's spirits soared, only to fall again to lower and lower levels with each disappointment. I met with the family daily, but as the days turned into weeks the daily updates changed little. Their resolute belief that I would find the answers, once quite gratifying, became a daily frustration and reminder of how little I knew of medicine.

As the specialists attempted their magic, I worked to protect Sol from the demons of the intensive care unit. Hospitals can be dangerous places. Often it's not the admitting illness that patients succumb to, but the inevitable complications that arise from intricate therapy in busy, understaffed units. Physical therapists worked with him daily to prevent the atrophy of unused muscles. An airbed was used to reduce the risk of bedsores. Pharmacists reviewed his medications daily, looking for possible drug interactions. Even the hospital chaplain made frequent trips to the bedside and the family waiting room.

After one month's time, Sol had been seen by twenty-four physicians and numerous nurses and therapists. He had received gallons of intravenous fluids, a pharmacy's worth of medication, and more X-rays than anyone could count. He remained in the intensive care unit, in the same room and the same bed. He remained in a coma.

The specialists had long given up and the prognostic statistics of unexplained coma provided no optimism. It was time to move Sol to an extended care facility and change from a focus of cure to one of support and comfort. It was a move that the family resisted, still confident of a miracle.

Late on a Friday afternoon I met with the family in the lounge just off the intensive care unit. We discussed Sol's condition at length, the opinions of the many consultants, and their own beliefs and desires. They accepted my recommendation that Sol be transferred the following Monday, knowing that the risk of further complications would be less at a nursing facility than in the hospital. They did not voice their disappointment, but I could see it in their eyes, and it left me with a sickening feeling. I don't believe that I had ever felt failure as intensely as I did that day. I knew I had let them all down.

The weather that evening was a reflection of my mood. It had been unseasonably warm for several days and an approaching cold front promised pleasant change, but first we would endure some difficult moments. Sitting in my darkened study, I hardly noticed the tree branches swaying against my window in the strong winds, or the ferocity of the lightning display that seemed to turn dark into day. I hardly cared when the power went out. They all seemed such trivial things.

Hours later I awoke with a start. "Nobody should die without steroids," a deep voice said.

I had been dreaming, but the dream seemed too vivid to be anything but reality. I was back in medical school. We were in our first weeks, a time of transition to a new life and bonding with classmates who would become lifelong friends. My new group of friends sat with me in the cafeteria during the lunch hour break, laughing hysterically at passages from a book that we had been passing around. The book had been written by a physician about his days in medical school. It was a satirical look at students and residents in a teaching hospital and brought levity into our stressful lives. Pearls of wisdom were summarized in "Rules of the House" and they became our rallying cry. One rule was that nobody should die without steroids. It didn't matter that no one knew what steroids were; it was a great line for medical students to carry around with them.

I fell back to sleep only to wake again with a clap of thunder that shook the house. The rain had started and water could be heard flooding down the roof and gutters. The wind continued to howl. I heard that voice again, "Nobody should die without steroids."

Hopes for a quiet Saturday morning at home faded when I noticed water in the basement. It wasn't a lot of water, but it would require immediate attention to salvage the boxes that sat in storage. The rain gauge had flowed over at four inches, and water was finding its way through a window well in the basement. I moved the half-dozen or so boxes out of harm's way and set about mopping the floor. It took an hour or so to divert the surface water away from the house, during which my curiosity about those boxes built. They were like mini time capsules. Most hadn't been opened in over a decade. I wondered what secrets they held.

I sat on the basement floor with my cup of coffee. I was late for rounds at the hospital, but certainly I had time for one quick peek. I came close to spilling my coffee when I opened the box closest to me. It was filled with texts, loose papers, framed diplomas, and on top, the book from my dreams the night before. If it was a coincidence, one had never unnerved me more. My hand trembled as I picked it up.

I found Sol Williams was unchanged when I arrived in the ICU. Expecting anything else would have been unrealistic, but still, I kept clinging to the slimmest of hope that one day he would show improvement. I ran into both the neurologist and infectious disease specialists during rounds and asked them each their thoughts about using steroids on Sol. After all, I rationalized, his labs did show evidence of inflammation when he was admitted. Both dismissed my suggestion as ludicrous, a product of inexperience and my desire to please the family. Nothing in the literature supported such a move.

It would not be a day of accomplishments. Every errand and domestic chore was preoccupied by thoughts of Sol and his family. I was certain that I had made the right decisions, but equally certain that if I had I would be feeling much better than I did. Falling into my easy chair by midafternoon, I rationalized a nap since I hadn't slept well the previous night. But my rest was fitful.

That book in the basement haunted me. Surrendering to its pull I retrieved it from my foggy past and returned to my study. Its cover was worn and the colors faded, but it fit in my hand like an old friend. Parting its pages, the book fell open to the words, "Nobody should die without steroids."

Reaching for the telephone, I called Sol's nurse in the ICU. I ordered the steroids.

In church Sunday morning, I received an urgent page from the ICU. I was asked to come immediately. I made it to the hospital in record time, fearing some catastrophic event the day before his transfer. Seeing the group of people gathered outside his room did nothing to reassure me as I rushed to his bedside. Sol was propped up with some pillows, his eyes open, looking rather amused about all the fuss around him.

While I had seen Sol every day for over a month, that Sunday was the first time we would actually meet. Sol was indeed transferred the following day, but to a rehabilitation center rather than a nursing home. Many years have passed since those anxious days, and Sol still comes to see me every few months, but his schedule is a busy one, filled with golf, bridge, and living a miracle.

CHAPTER 13

The Journey Home

When a great man dies, for years
the light he leaves behind him,
lies on the paths of men.
HENRY WADSWORTH LONGFELLOW

Betts Unger had died. She was ninety-four; it certainly wasn't unexpected news, and long ago I had come to the realization that part of her would forever be inseparable from me. Still, had I known, I would have liked to have traveled home for the funeral.

Saturday mornings always find memories in my mailbox. My hometown newspaper, published every Wednesday, usually catches up with me by week's end. While my links to that earlier time and place have grown tenuous through the years, the experiences I had and the lessons I learned there still walk with me. For a few minutes, I recall familiar places, follow old friends from school, and marvel at the changes in the town. It was in those pages that I learned of Betts's death.

It took me ten years to start calling her Betts. She was always Miss Unger to me, the English literature teacher at my high school. She taught there with her brother Christopher, the head of the English department. Neither having ever married, they shared a home together, and the community became their family. Their skill as birders was legendary in town, so much so that I couldn't wait to make it to high school as a boy. It took half of my freshman year to gain the courage to approach Miss Unger about my interest in birds, and she encouraged me politely. Somehow I had wanted more, and I was disappointed that I did not find it.

Every Sunday the Ungers went in search of birds at the marsh. One such morning in early spring, Miss Unger telephoned as I was preparing for church. Their usual birding companion could not accompany them that day, and I was invited in her place. I was excused from church that day to explore my dream.

It didn't take long to get hooked. The marsh and woods were mystical places and the birds that we found there were more beautiful than I had imagined possible. It was a potent narcotic, numbing the senses with awe and leaving a longing for more. But it was made up of more than the birds and the wild places. I was hooked on the Ungers.

Another invitation came the following Sunday, and then the next. Soon it was a given: Sundays were spent with the Ungers. My parents had some misgivings about the arrangement, concerned that I would be missing church. I think they knew, though, that what could be found in church, I would find with these two special people.

During the week they taught me English, the love of literature, and planted the seeds of the idea that one day I might write. During the weekends they taught me about birds, the love of nature, and reverence for silence. We made an unlikely trio: two aging schoolteachers and a teenager. During school breaks and summer vacation, we would travel to different parts of the country in search of birds. Wherever we went, they were mistaken for my grandparents. I think they liked that.

I found much more than birds on our travels together. I discovered places and people that energized me with incredible peace. It would be many years before I would start to understand just what that energy was, but my journey had started nonetheless, and Betts helped guide the way.

Since I learned of her passing, my thoughts have often turned to home. When I walk the hills of Appalachia, Betts walks with me. The quickening of my pulse upon sighting an uncommon bird, the exhilaration of the ephemeral wildflowers, and the tranquility of common beauty springs from that part of Betts that she shared with me and left behind. I have always felt her influence in my life, but since her death there has been more. I feel her presence.

Early one morning before dawn, home reached out to me again. Waking to a ringing telephone is seldom a good feeling. It means that either a patient has had an emergency that requires immediate attention, or that common sense is not common at all, and there was no need to wake up. Regardless, it was hard to get back to sleep. This call was particularly unsettling. It was Jean. Charles was having trouble breathing, and she didn't know what to do or who to call.

I'd known Jean and Charles, an aging couple from my hometown, all my life. In two decades of practice, I have watched many couples grow old and change, but it was hard to notice the changes in them, much like it's hard to notice aging in oneself. I told Jean to call 911. When she hung up the line, the silence left me with a bad feeling.

It was nearly two hours later that the telephone rang again. It was the emergency room doctor. Jean had asked him to call me. Charles had arrested by the time the paramedics reached him. They started CPR and took him to emergency. Soon he was on full life support, intubated, and on a ventilator. He was on pressors, medications to maintain his blood pressure. He was unresponsive and had no reflexes. It was a bad situation for an eighty-two-year-old man.

The emergency room doctor asked me if I knew what Charles would have wanted, noting that his wife didn't think they had living wills and that they had never discussed end-of-life issues. It was a question that shocked me into silence. I always discussed the topic with my patients. How could it be that I had never thought to bring it up with people close to me?

The phone would ring a third time before I was ready to start my day. The charge nurse at the ICU called to tell me that Charles had been admitted there. They wanted to know the best way to reach me, as Jean had asked that I be kept informed of his progress. I gave her the numerous numbers that kept me linked constantly to my work and thanked her for the courtesy.

"Doctor?" she asked as I was about to hang up the phone. "Were you trained here at the medical college?"

"Why, yes," I replied. "I went to medical school at the medical college. Why do you ask?"

"Dr. Berry was sure it must be you," she said. "He's the admitting cardiologist. The two of you were classmates in medical school. Dr. Daniel Berry?"

"Yes, I remember him well," I noted. "I haven't seen him since graduation."

"It's quite a coincidence," she raved. "Of the thousands of doctors, what are the odds of two classmates meeting by chance?"

What were the odds, indeed? The deeper my patients pulled me into their lives, the more obvious it became that there was no such thing as a random event. The quantum physicist understands it as chaos theory; that even in the randomness of total chaos there can be found great order, and also great beauty. Coincidence is an invention of the ego, to shield us from the possibility that some great organizing force is at work in the universe. What seems to be coincidental is only a reminder that this force is always at work, and if we seize upon the opportunities it offers us, our journey will be wondrous.

Dan Berry called me later that morning. There was little he could tell me that I didn't already know. Still, knowing what Charles looked like to him was important to me. It was, perhaps, my most valuable clinical tool. The answer was not good; Charles looked horrible. He was not going to survive. The problem was that modern medicine makes it difficult to die.

The office schedule was unusually heavy, but my staff had already started to free up time for me to get out of town. I told Dan that I could be there the following evening. Charles would be left on life support in the ICU. If he was going to get better, the time would provide him the opportunity. If not, then I would help the family with the difficult decisions that awaited them.

My heavy schedule in the office was made worse by moving up appointments for later in the week. Strangely, I didn't mind. It was good to be busy. At times my practice seemed more like an opportunity to visit with friends than care for patients. Many of my patients have been coming to see me for close to twenty years, and during that period of shared lives they have become family. Healing energy knows no direction. As it flows outward it also flows toward me, from those who have become my family.

The night before my trip home was restless. I couldn't get Helen Derickson out of my thoughts, or the message that she seemed to bring to me from some place beyond reasoning. I couldn't tell if the images I saw were dreams or simply my imagination. They both haunted and blessed my night.

Helen was sitting on a bench overlooking a tranquil pond. A great blue heron fished in the shallows as warblers hunted for morsels in the tangle of vines clinging to a hickory tree that shaded the bench. A Carolina wren worked at wild strawberries growing nearby. Betts Unger sat with her. She looked great; not as if she were ninety-four, but just as I had known her when we scouted the wilds for birds and the lessons to life. I cherished the opportunity that I thought I had lost to say goodbye. But Betts gave me a quizzical look; she hadn't gone anywhere, and she never would.

As Helen and Betts sat talking about birds, I took notice of the scene before me. It was familiar. It was the place where Betts, Christopher, and I used to eat lunch while birding. It was the site where my addiction was born, and the first place that I ever heard silence.

As I turned to leave, Helen spoke to me. "Remember what I told you, Bill," she said softly. "I will wait right here."

She smiled at my look of confusion and said, "It's time to solve the puzzle, Bill."

"What puzzle?" I asked.

"The journey that you're on," she said matter-of-factly. "You have all the pieces. Put them together."

I looked at the clock at my bedside. It was unchanged from the last time I had looked at it, but it seemed like I had been away for hours. That was how the night would pass. As fitful as it was, there was something refreshing about it, and I rose feeling rested, if more than a little apprehensive of the day to come.

By afternoon I was ready to start the trip home. Waiting for a train to pass, I sat in traffic next to a fire engine. As I scanned the controls I was taken back to an earlier time. The engine had both high-pressure and volume pumps, similar to what I had worked with so many years earlier. I wondered whether or not I could still operate it. Helen was right; I had been on a journey, one that seemed both long and far too brief. Looking back, the path is littered with memories, experiences, and bits of wisdom, like the pieces of a puzzle. That puzzle at the end of the journey could be nothing other than a life with meaning. It was on that drive home that the pieces would start to fall into place, the elements that make life meaningful.

The core of quantum physics and spirituality is the same: pure energy. It is only now that man has developed the technology to peer into the center of the universe, where infant galaxies are taking form. If at the origin of this creation the astrophysicist was surprised to find only energy, the spiritualist was not. Energy is the currency of the universe. With enough energy, there is no end to what can be obtained.

Everything is energy: objects, thoughts, actions, and, particularly relevant to the physician, healing. What else could explain the patients who enter the exam room feeling worried and fatigued, only to leave a few minutes later relieved and happy? Their body chemistry, anatomy, and even physiology all remain the same as they were before. Only their energy states are different.

People who visit a physician often feel better before the first pill is swallowed. The interaction is as important as, if not more than, the medication. Through that interaction passes energy. Illness, fatigue, worry, and pain are all low states of energy. Bring them in contact with a higher field of energy and inevitably these energy states rise; healing takes place. Compassion, happiness, optimism, empathy, and love are only a few of the higher forms of energy that can be taken into the examination room.

Fortunately for our patients, physicians do not need to understand healing energy for it to work. We just need to get out of the way and let it happen. Our understanding of nuclear fusion is irrelevant to the brightness of sunlight. Medical students are taught to smile and be happy around patients and avoid feelings of anger and frustration. We call it professionalism, but there is a better reason. Low energy states will block the flow of higher energy. All we are left with then is our science of medicine. Often that's not nearly enough.

You don't need to be a physician to make use of healing energy. Healing touch, acupuncture, and energy medicine all bring higher energy to diseased energy systems. Healing can even be accomplished independent of others. Meditation, prayer, yoga, and even faith can channel energy to where it is needed most. Erin was a master at manipulating energy. Of all the medications and treatments for her cancer, her attitude of optimism, service to others, and love proved the most potent, extending her survival ten years beyond the most optimistic predictions. But the energy she harnessed did not stop with her. She shared with others and they too were healed, their sadness and worry dissolved in the ease of her smile.

Learning to embrace the present moment was another piece of the puzzle. Helen Derickson came to believe in miracles. She noted that miracles happen in the now, and that you have to be there to experience them. Now is where all life occurs, both the miraculous and the ordinary. As you begin to savor the present moment, the distinction between the two becomes unimportant.

Helen lost much of her life to her past. It was a double tragedy. Her early years were not happy ones, filled with want and bitterness. Her later years were spent reliving the past, nourishing the bitterness and scarcity into lush anger and resentment. It was a perfect prison with infinite walls. The more she focused on the unhappiness of her past, the more unhappiness she found in the present, a guarantee that she would always be unhappy.

It wasn't until Helen was able to see her past for what it was, mere footprints in the sand, that she could see that she was standing on a beautiful beach. She learned to live her life where miracles take place, and found miracles most every day.

Karl Mannfeld lost much of his life to his future. His life was too busy with work and responsibility for him to see its beauty. That's what retirement was for. There would be time later for leisure, for beauty, and for family. Karl was standing on that same beach, but couldn't see the beauty any better than Helen could. He couldn't see the unmarked sand that stretched out before his feet. Instead, he focused on that distant island where someday he would travel.

Cancer saved Karl. It gave him a reason to look for life in the present moment. You only find what you look for, and in the present moment he found endless life. It will always be now. There will never be a time when it is not now; now is infinite. By choosing to experience every day, seize every opportunity, and savor every moment, Karl used his cancer to help him live an eternity.

Karl and Gretta found the present moment in the beauty of the German Alps. Some find it amid nature, others in the peace of silence. Still others find now through meditation, clearing of the mind of thought and sinking into the quiet of the soul. It was in that present moment that Karl experienced something curious, the peace and warmth of Spirit. It was something that he knew about, but did not know of. I experienced much the same phenomenon in the fire service.

Books and training drills provided me a knowledge about fire. But it was not until I experienced the heat on my face and the smoke in my lungs that I gained knowledge of fire. The energy of Spirit exists in the present, not in memories or dreams. Spirit is doing at this very moment what it has been doing for millennia: creating, nourishing, and healing. If we are unable to free ourselves from our past and resist the seduction of the future, we may come to know about Spirit, but never to know of Spirit. It took Karl a lifetime to find the present moment, and when he did, Spirit was waiting.

In every puzzle there is a piece that seems essential to understanding how the remainder of the picture will fall together. Forgiveness is one such piece, fitting snugly between energy and embracing the present moment. More often than not, we are unable to give up our past for a life in the present due to some transgression: a family's unfairness, a friend's betrayal, an unearned hatred, or even scarcity in our past. We become victims to the negative energy that enslaves us, unable to move forward in life.

That negative energy makes it difficult for higher energy to flow through us. Healing, peace, and even happiness are difficult to experience in this state, if not downright impossible. The antidote is forgiveness. Like all gifts, we benefit in giving forgiveness. Forgiving can be much more powerful than being forgiven.

Our egos do not make it easy for us to forgive, or even recognize what it is that we should forgive. Peter Marks sat in his wheelchair consumed with anger and hatred that he could not see. He had much to give others, but it remained locked inside him. It was not until he saw the hatred he had helped nurture in his nephew's heart that he could see his own. It was an awareness that came with an understanding of the need to forgive, and so he did.

Peter Marks forgave the man who shot him and put him in his chair. Through that act, Peter found the ability to serve others. He became a mentor and a role model. He experienced happiness. Perhaps the greatest change, however, was that instead of hatred, Peter showed his nephew what love was all about. It was the power of forgiveness.

If forgiveness opens the channel that allows energy to flow, gratitude is the environment from which energy grows. It is another one of the pieces of the puzzle. There are those among us who travel through life in a state of constant gratitude. It is a spiritual state. Those who practice it find uncommon peace and perpetual awe, as once gratitude is unleashed, it is impossible to contain. Being grateful for the big things in life is but a chip shot away from being grateful for the small things. Soon you feel gratitude for everything: the salesclerk that smiles, the smell of a fresh cut lawn, and the song of the Carolina wren. Every moment is a moment of gratitude.

Paul Prescot understood gratitude better than anyone. It was his spiritual fuel. It's easy to feel grateful when something good comes our way, but what about being grateful for hardship, for cancer? Paul found a way. He noted that the beauty of the sunrise comes only after the darkest part of the night. His cancer was an opportunity to learn and to teach others, and an opportunity to be grateful for the sunrise that was certain to follow.

Roger Harrold found gratitude in congestive heart failure. He could have done without the shortness of breath and the difficulty walking about his farm, but it gave him the opportunity to experience a depth of life that health had not. It brought him closer to his spirit and gave him more to leave behind to his family. It was a gratitude that accompanied him to his death.

The energy of our lives flows as service. Einstein noted, "The value of a man resides in what he gives and not in what he is capable of receiving." Ryan Charles recognized that the only thing we can do with our life is to give it away. Through service we find happiness. It's another piece of the puzzle. Just as the present moment is infinite, so are gratitude and service. You cannot give away something in the past, and a future gift is only a thought, not real giving. Once we learn to live our lives in the present moment, the opportunity to be of service to others is endless. You do not have to be a doctor in order to serve. The opportunity to give is far more abundant in ordinary life. A generous tip at a restaurant, a phone call answered with a pleasant voice, a cold can of soda pop for the trash collector, and keeping an eye out for the widow next door: an entire life can be spent in service, and in happiness.

I have come to see uncertainty as a friend, the type of friend who is willing to anger you in the effort to help you. Oddly enough, it is the last piece of the puzzle. For some, it is the most important piece, as it forces us to spend time in the present moment. No one is promised a tomorrow, and in the moment we recognize that, we find ourselves in the present moment—the time for miracles, gratitude, service, and happiness. Alex Kipton found uncertainty through death. It was the best thing that ever happened to him, not because he got a second chance for life, but because he began experiencing life for the first time. With the uncertainty of tomorrow, he learned to make use of each day, and in all of those days he found meaning and happiness.

Uncertainty touches us daily in medicine. The sudden heart attack, the diagnosis of cancer, the impact of a falling tree. Like the residents on the ward service, I struggled with such misfortune in my early years of practice. I still do, but now the struggle comes with the reminder that uncertainty is something that we must deal with along our journey. Now, I tend to put things off less often. I try to find good in people instead of anger, I look for beauty wherever I go, and I experience the quiet of peace every day.

Thomas, the medical student, noted that those who understood the physics of the universe the best became very spiritual people. It is humbling and strangely satisfying that the search for the origins of time has found only energy. So it has been with my practice. With every patient I understand the science of medicine a little bit better. The more I understand, the more I am left in awe, as my science is inadequate to explain the wonders that I have found. The answers have come from a special place, a place that few of us come to know. My patients know of this place: Peter Marks through forgiveness, Paul Prescot through service, Helen Derickson through embracing the present, Karl Mannfeld through accepting uncertainty, and Alex Kipton through seizing life from death. It is true. When the student is ready, the teacher will appear. Sometimes they appear even when we are not ready, and leave their lessons behind for another day.

Turning off the ignition, I glanced at my watch. I had over an hour before I was to meet the others at the hospital. Lost in thought, I found the trip had passed quickly. It was like waking from a dream and finding myself back home again. The car had been drawn to Second Street and I sat parked in front of Betts's home. She had spent the last year or two in a nursing home, but whoever lived there now hadn't changed a thing. A birdfeeder still hung from a tree outside her bedroom window, and a downy woodpecker worked hard to extract a sunflower seed from it. It would have delighted Betts, and I had a feeling that she was indeed watching with delight.

I had forgotten what it felt like to be home. The sense of peace seemed almost overwhelming, banishing the anxiety I had felt earlier about making the trip. In the blink of an eye decades had passed. I could see a boy standing on that porch, anxiously waiting for the door to open. On the other side of the door waited the exploration of nature, the discovery of spirituality, and friendship that reached across a generation. And while that boy was too young to understand it at the time, love also answered that door. The journey started on that porch.

I couldn't resist driving by the firehouse on the way to the hospital. Stopped across the street, I sat and watched the activity within. Tuesday night had always been drill night, the time when the department members gathered to practice skills and teach the younger members. All the trucks had been pulled out onto the apron to make room inside, lined up as if the bell had rung. I could see a young man standing beside one of those trucks, practicing at its controls. I could feel his excitement, as well as some fear that he closely guarded from the others. I could also feel his newfound joy: he was learning how to serve.

I hadn't been to the hospital since taking patients there as a paramedic. It was a small but well-equipped community hospital just across the river from my hometown. It was both familiar and strange. There had been remodeling through the years, but I knew right where the elevators were and how to get to the intensive care unit. I hadn't remembered it being so small, however. I peeked through the doors of the emergency room with some surprise. What I had remembered as a mammoth facility would fit into any one of three sections of the emergency department at the teaching hospital. How time and perspective changes our view of the world.

It had been five or six hours since I had last spoken with Dan Berry. Charles had not shown any improvement over the past day. In fact, there were new signs of renal failure. The dosage of medication that supported his blood pressure had been increased a number of times during the day. The neurologist saw little hope that he would ever regain consciousness. The pulmonologist felt certain that he would never come off the ventilator. But medicine had become very good at keeping old men alive on machines. Someday, its wisdom would catch up with its technology.

The family had gathered and was waiting for me in the ICU waiting room. I knew them all, and it felt good to see them. The sadness, however, tightened even my throat, and made words difficult to find. They all had questions. Jean worried that she had waited too long to call for help. His son wanted to know the reason for each medication that dripped into his father's veins. His granddaughters wanted to know if he was in pain.

We spent the better part of an hour talking about Charles. We discussed his philosophy on life and death. Not surprisingly, everyone had read the man the same. He loved life too much to see it pass this way.

As a group we went to his bedside. I couldn't help but see the fear in his granddaughters' eyes. I had become safely numb to the ICU, but its horrors were hard to hide from young people. They took some comfort in knowing the purpose for each piece of equipment, but they were appalled to find their grandfather in such a lifeless place. They even expressed some doubt that the man who lay in the bed was their grandfather.

Indeed, Charles did not look good. His eyes were dark, and the aura of life was missing. His chest rose and fell with the cycling of the ventilator, and the tube that connected the machine to his airway seemed uncomfortably large. Eight IV bags hung around his bed, almost like vultures perched in wait. The only sign of life was that shown on the digital displays of the computerized monitor. His blood pressure was low, and his heart beat rapidly.

I looked about the room with an uncomfortable feeling of familiarity. While every ICU looks different, I felt that I had been in this one before. The wall was covered with get-well wishes, just as Helen Derickson's room had been. Strange that I would feel her presence so strongly in this place.

I stepped out into the hall to speak with the nurse caring for Charles. She reported that he had stopped making urine and his cardiac rhythm had become irregular.

"What are your orders?" I asked.

Her smile was so warm that it took the chill from the room. "Dr. Berry told me to do whatever you asked me to do," she said, gently placing her hand on my shoulder. Together, we returned to Charles's bedside.

It was difficult to wait there while everyone said their good-byes to Charles. I asked the nurse to slowly turn off the intravenous medications that were supporting his blood pressure. His blood pressure gradually fell, and his heart rate became progressively slower. All eyes became fixed to the monitor. Heads would bob with every beat of the heart. As the heads bobbed slower and slower, I had the nurse turn off the monitor. A few minutes and a nod later, she turned off the ventilator.

I had thought that my journey through the fire service, medical school, residency, and years of practice had prepared me for everything, but it hadn't prepared me for that moment. The journey was not over. With tears in my eyes I put my arm around my mother as my brother placed his around me. The peace that I had missed from my father's face had returned.

It was a slow walk back to my car. I had parked in the far corner of the hospital lot, near a grove of trees and a couple of picnic tables. No doubt it was a popular place for hospital employees to eat dinner. The sun was setting, casting long shadows in its golden light. Perched on a branch of a maple tree, not more than a foot from me, was a Carolina wren. I had never come so close to one, and I was mystified by its lack of concern with my presence. I could see the individual feathers on its face.

In that magical light of sunset, the Carolina wren tilted back its head and sang with rare splendor. In the reflection in its eye, I was certain that I could see a tranquil pond. Overlooking the pond was a bench where Helen sat. She had waited, and Betts sat with her. Between them sat my father.